The Reminiscences

of

Mrs. Marc A. Mitscher

and

Mrs. Roy C. Smith, Jr.

U.S. Naval Institute
Annapolis, Maryland
1986

Preface

Understandably, much of naval history deals with the achievements of the men—officers and enlisted—who operate ships and aircraft and serve at shore stations around the world. There is obviously more to the story than just the exploits of these men, for in many cases they received a great deal of support and assistance from their wives. While the men were off engaging the enemy or helping to train the fleet during peacetime, it was left to their wives to run the households, care for the children, move the families frequently, and to put up with the long separations and inconveniences that are a part of Navy life.

The two memoirs in this volume are, coincidentally, both from the widows of officers who were graduated in the Naval Academy's class of 1910. Even so, they are strikingly different in tone. Mrs. Marc Mitscher provides a wife's-eye view of one of the U.S. Navy's most famous admirals of World War II. In so doing, she reveals facets of his personality that only she saw. She recognizes that he was a different man at home than on board ship, and she describes the portion of his life that she shared. As a by-product, one gains a realization of the large degree that her life was shaped by her relationship with Marc Mitscher. She went where his career dictated, and thus her interests were dictated largely by her husband's interests.

Mrs. Roy C. Smith, Jr., addresses the theme of dependency to an even larger degree than does Mrs. Mitscher. With a wry sense of humor, Mrs. Smith dwells on the inconveniences that go with raising a Navy family at home and abroad. She had to find solutions to a good many problems that don't confront a civilian homemaker rearing children entirely in the United States. One reads here about difficulties in dealing with the cultures in such places as China and Panama and the ways in which her children got into the sort of scrapes that children inevitably do. In addition to being a Navy wife and a Navy mother, Mary Smith was also a Navy daughter. Her earliest recollections in this oral history extend back to the beginning of the 20th century when she was living on the grounds of the Naval Academy, where her father was a professor and an early secretary-treasurer of the Naval Institute. In her charming fashion, Mrs. Smith describes the simplicity of an era long since past---a time before telephones and automobiles were common and when radio and television had yet to be invented.

Thanks go to Dr. John Mason, Jr., former director of the Naval Institute's oral history program, and to Commander Etta-Belle Kitchen, a retired naval officer, for conducting the interviews which comprise this volume. Ms. Susan Sweeney supplied the detailed annotation of the transcript and the excellent index. Captain Roy C. Smith III, USNR(Ret.), provided useful information in preparing his mother's transcript for publication in this form. Mrs. Deborah Reid did the transcription and typing of the volume.

                                                Paul Stillwell
                                                Director of Oral History
                                                U.S. Naval Institute
                                                May 1986

Frances Smalley Mitscher was born on 25 October 1890 in Tacoma, Washington, the daughter of attorney and judge Francis A. Smalley. She married Ensign Marc Andrew Mitscher, USN (Naval Academy class of 1910) on 16 January 1913 at Trinity Episcopal Church in Tacoma. The Mitschers had no children. Admiral Mitscher was born in Hillsborough, Oklahoma, on 26 January 1887, and died while serving as Commander in Chief Atlantic Fleet on 3 February 1947 in the Naval Hospital at Norfolk, Virginia. Mrs. Mitscher died in a nursing home in Coronado, California, on 20 December 1982, and is buried beside her husband in Arlington National Cemetery.

Mary Taylor Alger Smith was born on 1 May 1892 in Washington, D.C., the daughter of naval officer Philip R. Alger and the former Louisa Taylor. She married Ensign Roy Campbell Smith, Jr., USN (Naval Academy class of 1910) on 1 August 1912 at her mother's home in Annapolis. The Smiths had four children, Roy Campbell III (born 14 May 1913), Mary Alger (born 22 June 1915), Louisa Taylor (born 27 April 1917), and Montgomery Meigs (born 1 April 1919). Commander Smith, born in the quarters of the Naval Academy Superintendent (his grandfather) on 1 August 1888, retired from the Navy with a physical disability in 1938, and died on 1 June 1946 in the Naval Hospital at Newport, Rhode Island. Mrs. Smith currently lives with her daughter, Mary Staley, in Newport. A comprehensive Smith family history was researched by her son, Montgomery, and his wife, and completed in 1982.

DECLARATION OF TRUST

The undersigned does hereby appoint and designate as his (her) Trustee herein, the Secretary-Treasurer and Publisher of the United States Naval Institute to perform and discharge the following duties, powers, and privileges in connection with the possession and use of a certain taped interview between the undersigned and the Oral History Department of the United States Naval Institute.

(1) As an <u>Open</u> transcript. It may be read (or the tape audited) by qualified researchers upon presentation of proper credentials as determined by the Trustee.

(2) It is expressly understood that in giving this authorization, I am in no way precluded from placing such restrictions as I may desire upon use of the interview at any time during my lifetime, nor does this authorization in any way affect my rights to the copyright of any literary expressions that may be contained in the interview.

Witness my hand and seal this ___1st___ day of ___May___ 19_71_.

Frances S. Mitscher

I hereby accept and consent to the foregoing Declaration of Trust and the powers therein conferred upon me as Trustee:

_____
Secretary-Treasurer and Publisher

Authorization

The U.S. Naval Institute is hereby authorized to make available to libraries and other repositories of its choosing the transcripts of two oral history interviews concerning the life of the undersigned. The two interviews were recorded on 24 March and 23 October 1978 in collaboration with Dr. John T. Mason, Jr. of the Naval Institute.

The undersigned does hereby release and assign to the U.S. Naval Institute all right, title, restrictions, and interest in these two interviews. The copyright in both the oral and transcribed versions shall be the sole property of the U.S. Naval Institute. The tape recordings of the interviews are and will remain the property of the U.S. Naval Institute.

Signed and sealed this ___14th___ day of __February__ 1985.

_____
Mary A. Smith (Mrs. Roy C. Smith, Jr.)

Interview Number 1 with Mrs. Frances Smalley Mitscher

Place: Mrs. Mitscher's home in Coronado, California

Date: 23 January 1971

Subject: Admiral Marc A. Mitscher, U.S. Navy

Interviewer: Commander Etta-Belle Kitchen, U.S. Navy (Retired)

Q: I should say that in Mrs. Mitscher's home we are surrounded with beautiful things and with wonderful memories of the admiral. It's an inspiration to see them, Mrs. Mitscher, and I appreciate the opportunity.

I'm sure the Institute will be happy to have your comments relating to the admiral. You have told me that he didn't comment too much on military matters. Would you like to amplify on that?

Mrs. Mitscher: That's true, and, as I said, I didn't see too much of him after he came home; he was still away a lot. Once in a while, he might say something but not really very much because he was very tired. I will say that we were sort of pursued by people, so that it was difficult for me to have much time with him, which you know how it goes under those circumstances.

Q: When he came back from the Pacific, what date was that?

Mrs. Mitscher: It was early in July of '45, just before the war was over.

Q: And where did you go when he returned? What were his duties then?

Mrs. Mitscher: We went to Washington. I think we were there about three weeks or a month before we went to the Navy Department. He relieved Admiral Fitch.*

Q: Was that the time he went on a speaking tour?

Mrs. Mitscher: Yes. He relieved Admiral Fitch. We were there that period of time, I think, about six months, before we went down to the fleet in Norfolk.

Q: Did he find the speaking easy?

Mrs. Mitscher: No, he said it was the hardest thing that he had ever done. Of course, I, as well as anybody who knew him, knew he wouldn't choose that to do.

Q: Was he on radio and TV also?

Mrs. Mitscher: He was on TV, and I think radio also.

---

*Vice Admiral Aubrey W. Fitch, USN, who was relieved by Mitscher as Deputy Chief of Naval Operations (Air) in July 1945.

Q: And he found those difficult assignments?

Mrs. Mitscher: Yes. I know that the one time that I did go when he was speaking in New York, he didn't have any makeup on for the television, and the man that was interviewing him did have, so it was quite a contrast.

Then, of course, he was gone a great part of that six months. Then we went to Norfolk, and he was at sea again. I know he hadn't been there very long when he went over to Europe. He flew over with Admiral Forrest Sherman.*

Q: He did not live too long after the war, did he?

Mrs. Mitscher: No.

Q: Did you ever feel that the war contributed to the shortness of his life?

Mrs. Mitscher: He was very thin when he came home, and at times he didn't seem too well, but I really did not know. I think sometimes there was sort of an instinctive fear in me that he wasn't very well, but I don't think I really wanted to admit it

---

*On 19 August 1946, Admiral Mitscher, Vice Admiral Forrest P. Sherman, USN, and Commodore Arleigh A. Burke, USN, left on a tour of European naval installations. In September Mitscher was forced to return to the United States after an emergency operation for appendicitis.

to myself.

Q: Did you ever ask him about it?

Mrs. Mitscher: No. He always said he was all right. This feeling that I had, I must say, was really a short time before he was gone. I realized that I had a nervousness about him that I hadn't had before.

Q: Did he indicate that he didn't feel well?

Mrs. Mitscher: No, except that he was tired, that he didn't want to go out very much. Of course, when we arrived in Washington we did go a lot, but he seemed to be very well then.

When he first came home from the flight to the Mediterranean, and after the appendectomy, he seemed to be just fine. He put on some weight and looked just wonderful.

Q: He had an emergency appendectomy?

Mrs. Mitscher: That was on the way back, in Malta, I think, when he was with the Atlantic Fleet.

Q: I think it would be interesting to go back to your early days with the admiral. Of course, he wasn't the admiral then. Tell me when you met him, and under what circumstances.

Mrs. Mitscher: I met him at the wedding of my closest friend. We were very young, 18 and 19. I visited her a few months later with her husband in Bremerton, and there I met him again.*

The ship that he was on, the Colorado, was going out to the Asiatic. He asked me if I would come to dinner with him in Seattle before leaving. Then he wrote me and invited me to come to the ship to dinner, which I did. Then he left for the Orient, and on the way out he wrote and asked me to marry him.

Q: So you had only seen him how many times?

Mrs. Mitscher: About three times.

Q: And he asked you to marry him?

Mrs. Mitscher: Yes.

Q: I think that is amusing in the sense that one pictures him as a retiring person, but he wasn't in this case, was he?

Mrs. Mitscher: No. The night of the dance that I went to in

---
*Bremerton, Washington, was the site of the Puget Sound Navy Yard.

Bremerton, every time I stopped dancing he stood beside me, and the young man I was with wouldn't give him a dance. That's when he asked me if I would come to the ship to dinner, and then he wrote to me. This was in Seattle, but I lived in Tacoma. I was staying with a friend.

He was only a passed midshipman at that time, and not allowed to marry.*

Q: He had to go to sea two years then, didn't he, before he became an ensign?

Mrs. Mitscher: Yes, he was out there at least two or three years before he came back.

When he came back he changed duty with a classmate in San Francisco, whose wife was expecting a baby, and he went down to Mexico on a gunboat, where in a very short time he transferred ships. So he didn't come back from there, down in Mexico, for at least another year.

When he came back, the ship was in dry dock in San Francisco. He had a month's leave and came to Tacoma and stayed at a hotel for a month. That was renewing our acquaintance.

Q: You hadn't told me how you answered his question.

---
*Mitscher was graduated from the Naval Academy in 1910 and was a passed midshipman from then until he was commissioned an ensign in 1912.

Mrs. Mitscher: I don't remember. I was amused by it at the time; I didn't take it very seriously. I was 19. I didn't take it seriously enough. I did write to him, and continued to write to him. And wrote some to the other chap as well.

Then he came to the hotel and stayed a month, and was very serious about this. He had to go back to the ship and was going back to Mexico and expected to be gone for another six months.

I told him that was fine, I would consider myself engaged to him until he came back six months later.

He got back to the ship and found there was to be a delay. So without getting in touch with me, he got on the train and wired me that he was arriving. And that he only had one week to stay and that we would have to be married then.

Of course, I didn't think it was possible, but at the end of the week we were married.

Q: That almost makes him sound impetuous, doesn't it?

Mrs. Mitscher: I don't know. He knew what he wanted to do.

My father said to me, when he wired that he was coming back, "Now you see the trouble you're in? I knew it when I looked at that boy's jaw."

Q: About the word impetuous, I would say that he had only a one-track mind and from the time he saw you, he didn't change.

Mrs. Mitscher: When he came back and came up there to Seattle, his mother and father came out. I still was not taking this very seriously.

I never regretted it.

Q: How would you have described him then? What did you think of his characteristics in those days, if you were thinking along those lines?

Mrs. Mitscher: I was too young to think about it very much. I always teased him and told him it was because he had so much stronger will than I did.

Then, of course, he went off to Mexico immediately after we were married. For the next three years, until he went into aviation, we altogether had never been together except three months at different times--one time he had a month's leave--until he went to Pensacola in flying. Which he had always been asking for on his record, but had really given up the idea that they were ever going to give it to him.

He finally went on a destroyer and went up to Alaska. Then, when he came back, he had a telegraph with orders to Pensacola in aviation. That was in October of 1915.

Q: Where did you stay during those three years?

Mrs. Mitscher: I used to know how many times I'd gone up and down the coast every time he came back. I stayed in Seattle most of the time with a married sister. My life wasn't changed very much at that period, because I'd only been with him such a short time. I still had my young friends, some of them were married, some were not.

Q: What was he like then?

Mrs. Mitscher: Being separated almost immediately, I didn't know.

Q: Did you think of him as being gay or serious? Did he laugh very much?

Mrs. Mitscher: I don't think so in those days. I think he was greatly distressed over so much separation. As I say, I didn't know him until later years, when we had a chance to really get some time together.

Q: When he went to Pensacola, that was the first opportunity to actually have a home?

Mrs. Mitscher: Yes, to be in one place. We were there a year and a half.

Q: Did he ever talk to you about why he wanted to be an aviator?

Mrs. Mitscher: No, he didn't say why, except that he wanted to be, and wanted very much to go into aviation.

Of course, when he came back, in those short periods of time he had the duty a lot. We'd go out to dinner and enjoy ourselves. Most of the time it would be a weekend or a few days, and then he'd be gone again.

Q: What was he like around home?

Mrs. Mitscher: We were always in a hotel; we didn't have a home.

Q: When you were at Pensacola?

Mrs. Mitscher: We had to live most of the time there in a hotel. It was a navy yard that had just been opened and made into the Pensacola training station. Henry Mustin was in command of it.[*]

There weren't many places to rent in those days, and we didn't have furniture that we took around like things are today.

There I made my first friends in the service--Mrs. Mustin she was then, and later after Captain Mustin died, she married

---

[*]Lieutenant Commander Henry C. Mustin, USN, Naval Aviator #11.

Admiral Murray.* So our lives went together always; we were very close friends.

In those early days of aviation, there were so few of us, and so few aviators, that we all wandered around together in Washington or out here, so there was a group that knew each other very well.

Q: Were you able to be with him much after Pensacola?

Mrs. Mitscher: Yes, except in the Second World War. He went first on the San Diego, I think, on a convoy, but when he came back he was ordered down to command the training station in Miami, Florida.

Q: Let me go back a bit. What number was it, in aviation?

Mrs. Mitscher: Thirty-three.

Q: Can you describe the life around Pensacola at that time?

Mrs. Mitscher: It was a very pleasant life, very attractive people, and the sort of life that you would live in a small town and in a navy yard. We really enjoyed ourselves very much. Of

---
*After Captain Mustin's death in August 1923 due to an aortic aneurysm, his widow, Corinne, married Naval Aviator #22, George D. Murray, who retired as a four-star admiral in 1951.

course, he learned to fly, and he was busy. We were together for that whole year and a half.

Q: Did he seem to love aviation, flying?

Mrs. Mitscher: He was very dedicated, but again I say he was not a man who talked about himself or what went on. He wasn't that sort of person.

Q: What did you talk about when you were together?

Mrs. Mitscher: Many things. I became the talker of the family, really, which I hadn't been too good at. He was a man who liked his close friends and small parties. He was a very good host.

We had a very close association. We didn't quarrel, except for the small quarrels that I suppose any married couple has, but I don't think we did have any. I would have quarreled, but he never would.

Q: He sounds as though he were an easy man to live with.

Mrs. Mitscher: Very, a very gentle man and very generous. It's hard to describe him, because I was a little while understanding him. Whether I did or not, I can't answer. We became very close. And he became a wonderful person to me. It always seemed to me that I really grew up under him. I had such a wonderful feeling of respect for him. He could be lots of fun. I never knew when he was teasing me. He could tell me something with a completely straight face.

Q: Do you have any recollection of any of those instances?

Mrs. Mitscher: Yes, I have one. When the Akron crashed, we were packing up to come out here on sea duty, and so were the Cecils.* Then, of course, he was killed on the Akron. We motored out, and I was very tired when we left Washington. We were not talking very much, either one of us. We finally were going through Kansas.

He said, "We have to get through Kansas in one day." I thought I won't ask him, I'm too tired, why he has to get through Kansas in one day. Then he said, "If a tremendous black cloud comes up over there, it's probably a cyclone. If we stop the car, just lie down and grab hold of something." And I didn't see anything out there to take hold of. We got into Colorado late that night.

The next day I said, "Why did we have to get through Kansas in one day?"

---

*The rigid airship Akron (ZRS-4) crashed in a storm off Barnegat Light, New Jersey, on 4 April 1933. Among the 73 fatalities were Rear Admiral William A. Moffett, USN, Chief of the Bureau of Aeronautics, and Commander Henry B. Cecil, USN.

And he said, "Why, no beer." I could have strangled him. He had a great keen sense of humor, very puckish sense of humor, too. He could be a lot of fun.

Q: Do you remember any stories he enjoyed telling?

Mrs. Mitscher: He never told stories very much. I'm sure he did with the men. You mean stories about his own experiences?

Q: No. You said he was a nice host--stories that he would tell in a group.

Mrs. Mitscher: No, I don't think so. Our life was quite busy, and it's been a long time. I still say he wasn't a man who talked very much about himself. I think when he was with the men he probably did more than he did when it was mixed.

Q: Some of the adjectives one reads of him, among them is "taciturn." Would you use that term as relating to him?

Mrs. Mitscher: They have used that so much. As I said to Admiral Burke, I think it's almost impossible for me to tell somebody what he was like as a man, because I only knew him as a husband.

Q: I don't know whether that's a more important aspect of his life or not, but how would you evaluate his position as husband as importance to him?

Mrs. Mitscher: I didn't know him as a man fighting a war, and I didn't know him as he was out fishing or hunting with men. I knew him as a very substantial, honest, generous, and wonderful husband.

Q: How do you think he evaluated his position as a husband to his wife as being an important facet of his life?

Mrs. Mitscher: I really wouldn't know how to answer that. I can tell you of one little incident--I live in the past--that came to me very recently.

One day there were a group of people sitting around talking. I can't remember why the subject came up--of what a person decided was the most beautiful thing to them that they had known of. When they asked my husband, he said, "Hearing a woman's voice speak the marriage service."

There was a very sort of shocked and dead silence in the room; everybody, I think was quite surprised. I can see that scene very well. That was in about 1922 or 1923.

Q: That must have been a touching experience for you.

Mrs. Mitscher: Yes, it was.

Q: I don't read of there being children.

Mrs. Mitscher: No children.

Q: Do you think that made you closer?

Mrs. Mitscher: I lost a baby before the full time during the First World War. At that time, they were sort of numbered as to when they would go abroad during the war. We were in New York. He was working on the building of the air station at Rockaway. He was ordered to go to Miami to command the training station, and he didn't know when he might leave. So he wanted me to go home, which I did.

I argued this a little bit, but he did want me to go home. I lost the baby between six and seven months, was very ill, and almost lost my life. I was never able to have any more children.

Q: Did he explain why he wanted you to go home?

Mrs. Mitscher: He was afraid that I'd be left alone on the East Coast if he went abroad. This probably is characteristic.

I lost the baby in May, and I went to Miami, where he still was in command, in August. From that time until the rest of his life, he never once mentioned the subject to me that we were even going to have a baby.

Q: Did he seem to like children?

Mrs. Mitscher: Oh, very much. He was very different, and, as I say, through the years it took a little knowing him.

Q: Could you tell when he was cross?

Mrs. Mitscher: I can't really remember his ever being cross with me. I suppose he must have been. I know there are things he'd say he didn't want me to do.

I'd seen him angry one time on the air station in Miami when something happened, but he always controlled himself. He kept everything inside of him. I think that did his health more damage probably during the war, because I knew he suffered over the loss of the young men's lives. Everything was kept within him.

Q: You say that he told you some things he didn't want you to do. Do you have any recollection . . .

Mrs. Mitscher: I meant some minor incident or something that might come up in ordinary living. I don't remember anything specific. I don't remember his ever being really angry with me. I'm sure that he was, but he didn't show it.

Q: Did you ever get angry with him?

Mrs. Mitscher: Oh, yes, of course.

Q: What did he do to make you angry?

Mrs. Mitscher: Oh, I don't know, probably some minor thing that I would want him to do, nothing of great importance. As I say, he never would fight with me.

Q: What did he like to eat? Did he have any special likings?

Mrs. Mitscher: He liked very good food, but he ate very little. He didn't care for desserts, but he liked very well cooked and very good food, but he never ate very much.

His mother was such a marvelous cook. I never ever experienced anything like that, and I don't think she did much cooking until later in her life when she thought of writing a cookbook. One of the things she made was a noodle soup, which she made the noodles for, and I learned to make the noodles. He was very fond of chicken and noodle fricassee. Other than that, just ordinary things, but he liked well cooked food. Of course, he liked game; he would shoot duck.

Q: Was he a sportsman?

Mrs. Mitscher: Yes. He loved fishing. He didn't particularly want to shoot a deer, but he did shoot in Alaska. I don't know whether he ever shot a deer or not, because I know he didn't really want to do that; he wasn't too anxious to.

Q: Would he say that to you? How did you know that?

Mrs. Mitscher: Yes, he said so. After the war when he went to the King Ranch in Texas and they were shooting, the host said to him, "You really don't want to shoot a deer, do you?"

And he said, "No, I don't."

Q: It would seem he had a respect for life.

Mrs. Mitscher: I should think it would be sort of hard. I'm sure he might have at some time.

Last Saturday was my 58th anniversary, so it's a long period of time.

Q: And in three days it would be his birthday. He was born on the 26th.*

Did he ever have any opportunity to talk about his philosophy of life and death? Did he have a feeling of religious sense, or do you recall?

Mrs. Mitscher: He was not a churchgoer. I'm sure he had his own feelings about religion. But neither one of us were church-going people.

Q: I wasn't thinking so much of a form of religious attitude, but perhaps his philosophy about people and life.

Mrs. Mitscher: I'm sure he had one, but I couldn't really know.

Q: Do you know if he thought when someone died that that was it, or did he express any thoughts on that?

Mrs. Mitscher: He never expressed an opinion on it. Of course, there were so many killed in aviation. I said to him one time—to please not ask me to have him cremated. Why the conversation came up, he had said that if he were killed he would haunt me if I ever let anybody ever look at him in a coffin.

When we were here one time when so many of them were killed in a short period of time, I asked him not to ask me to have him

---

*Admiral Mitscher was born on 26 January 1887 and married Frances Smalley on 16 January 1913.

cremated because I was not able at that time. I might change my mind in later years, but at that time I would not be able to do it. That's the only conversation that I remember that we ever had on the subject.

Q: What did he say, when you said that?

Mrs. Mitscher: I don't know whether he even answered me or not. I assured him that I would not have the coffin open for anybody to look at him.

When we were going from Norfolk up in the plane when he died, they gave me this list. They said he would lie in state, and I asked them if that's what it meant and they said yes. I told them it could not be done.

Q: I can understand your feeling on that. Do you recall him ever being interested in what you wore, or how you looked?

Mrs. Mitscher: Yes, to some extent. Like most men, he didn't really. I always knew if he didn't like something, because he'd say, "Haven't you had that a long time?"

One time I remember I had a hat that he didn't like, so I never wore it. But ordinarily I'm sure he didn't particularly notice what I had on. He'd let me know if he didn't like it, I guess.

Q: I think you're so pretty that he probably didn't much care. I'm sure you looked lovely in anything.

Mrs. Mitscher: I think they know if they don't like something, but otherwise I think most men are like that.

Q: Did he tell you often that you were pretty?

Mrs. Mitscher: I suppose he must have.

Q: Was he interested in home decorating?

Mrs. Mitscher: Yes, he was very much interested in our home. Sometimes when I had a party, he would compliment me on the dinner, that I always did it very well. As I say, he liked good food.

Q: What were his other activities? You spoke of his going fishing and hunting for game?

Mrs. Mitscher: Yes. We played golf together quite a lot. He was a good golfer, he didn't pretend to play an expert game. I played golf before he did. I was taking lessons; this was in Pensacola. There was a group of young people playing golf.

So one Sunday he said he would go out and walk around with

me. He wanted to see what I was doing. Halfway around he said, "Give me one of those clubs." And that's the way he started to play golf; he never took a lesson.

Q: Was he instinctively a good athlete?

Mrs. Mitscher: They thought at the Naval Academy, he told me, that he was going to be a very good baseball player. But something happened to his arm; it would go out of joint.

He wrestled at the Naval Academy. That's the only sport that I know of. He played, I've been told, football in high school, and that sort of thing. But you wouldn't call him an athlete, no.

Q: Was he interested in music or artistic things? Did he have time for it?

Mrs. Mitscher: No, I wouldn't say that he had any particular interest. He would go--he loved the theater. We went to the theater together; he loved that. He did go to concerts with me. If I wanted to go, he would go, and I suppose he enjoyed them. He enjoyed the ballet when we went. He enjoyed musical comedy and things of that sort.

Q: He liked plays--any particular type that he preferred?

Mrs. Mitscher: No, he just liked good theater.

Q: You have so many beautiful things that I thought perhaps he had collected some of them.

Mrs. Mitscher: No. In this house, in this room, half of the things were mine and half of the things were inherited with the house. I started a small figurine collection when I was young. Not having any children, I was interested in antiques and things of that sort and occupied myself that way. And he was very pleased to have me to do it. He had that much interest in it, liked his home and enjoyed it very much.

Q: He didn't really have much time to be in it, did he?

Mrs. Mitscher: We had several shore duties in Washington, D.C., which were wonderful.

Q: What were your living arrangements there, an apartment?

Mrs. Mitscher: Yes, we lived in an apartment because he was away quite often. We lived in the same apartment building three different times, and I had an apartment that I liked very much. I had my own things then.

When we went back there after the First World War, it was

very difficult to get a place to live. We had a small apartment. You rented furnished apartments, but they were so awful I couldn't see living there. So I furnished a small apartment, and from then on we had our own things. When we came out of Washington, I always stored them there, when he went to sea.

Q: Did he smoke?

Mrs. Mitscher: Yes--much too much--cigarettes. He smoked a lot. The first thing in the morning when he woke up, he always awakened at dawn, you could hear the cigarette being lighted. He inhaled very deeply and smoked very little of the cigarette, but many of them.

Q: He drank coffee, I presume.

Mrs. Mitscher: Yes, I wouldn't say he was a tremendous coffee drinker, not as much as I was.

Q: What about drinking? Did he enjoy having a cocktail?

Mrs. Mitscher: Yes, he enjoyed it very much. We always had a cocktail every night before dinner.

Q: I want to go back to the word "taciturn" which people did use about him.

Mrs. Mitscher: I suppose he was, really, to the public but not with his close friends. I couldn't know what he was like aboard ship.

Q: Did he ever discuss politics? Did you know if he had an interest in politics?

Mrs. Mitscher: He had the interest that we all had, but, of course, we didn't have a vote. It so happened that we had shore duty every time in Washington, D.C., and we didn't have a vote. We didn't live anyplace long enough to have a vote. If we had voted, I'm sure he would have voted Republican ticket. We were interested, and always interested in the elections but neither one could vote. I didn't until I came out and lived here.

Q: What about some of the people you met? You must have met some awfully interesting people in your years with the admiral.

Mrs. Mitscher: Of course I did, especially when he came back in '45. As I say again, I was with him very little of that time.

I knew Admiral Burke, and loved them both very dearly. They're like some of my family now. Of course, I didn't know him until he came back from the Pacific with my husband. Mrs. Burke and I are very close friends.

Mrs. Mitscher: Did you ever have a chance to know Admiral Nimitz?*

Mrs. Mitscher: Over a period of years, meeting at parties, but never a close association. We were never right where they were.

Q: What about Admiral Halsey?**

Mrs. Mitscher: I didn't know him well at all. We weren't together either. When I was quite young here in the early Twenties, I think they were here for a short time and I met them. But again we weren't on duty with them.

William Augustus Read was on Admiral Mitscher's staff out in the Pacific.*** When we came back, they so wonderfully invited us up there very frequently, and then we went up to Canada on a salmon fishing trip with them. Of course, he and my husband had been together for some time. I had met him just casually in Washington, and then when I met Mrs. Read we became friends and have continued to be so through the years.

Following my husband's death, they both were wonderful to me. He was so wonderful in helping me in every way and would not let

---
*Fleet Admiral Chester W. Nimitz, USN.
**Fleet Admiral William F. Halsey, USN.
***Rear Admiral William A. Read, USN.

very much go by without calling to see how I was getting along. It's one of those things that is appreciated so much that you couldn't possibly ever forget it.

Q: How long did you stay in the East before you came back to Coronado?

Mrs. Mitscher: Two years and a half.

Q: The days when Admiral Mitscher became an aviator he was one of the early people. Were you aware of the black shoe-brown shoe conflict at that time?*

Mrs. Mitscher: No, not in those early days in Pensacola, at least I wasn't. That seemed to come up later. Of course, it was such a small group of people at that time, very few aviators at that time.

Q: Did you ever feel any antagonism from people who weren't aviators against the aviators, because they got more pay or because they were an elite group?

Mrs. Mitscher: I think there was that to some extent. Even

---

*Aviators are known as "brownshoes" and surface ship officers as "blackshoes."

today I have experiences, but that came along a little bit later.

Q: Did it ever have any unpleasantness for you?

Mrs. Mitscher: No. I knew it existed. But I say again, we were a close little group of people, very close friends.

Q: He was in a troop convoy in World War I. You did go down and join him in Miami, and how long was he there before he left during World War I?

Mrs. Mitscher: I joined him in Miami in August. The armistice came in November, and then we went on to Washington. He went on to transatlantic flying.

Q: Can you tell me any incidents relating to that?

Mrs. Mitscher: He went up to Rockaway to oversee getting the planes ready, as I remember it, long before there was any publicity about it at all.

A friend of mine whose husband was a doctor in the armed forces in Europe hadn't come back yet. She and her mother and small child were there and had an apartment in Brooklyn. So I went over and lived there in an apartment in the same building, and he was out at Rockaway.

Then when the flight took place, after the NC-4 arrived there, they all went over to Europe.* When they were coming home, I got a telephone call to be at the 90th Street dock to go out on a yacht to meet the ship that was coming in that was bringing the fliers home. I did, and when I got there very early, they had all left.

It seems that the admiral's aide in Brooklyn called up the apartment to tell that there had been a change. This five-year-old child answered the telephone and he gave her the message. When I got home, she said that she thought it was somebody we knew that had called, that the hour had been set up an hour ahead of time. So you can imagine my feelings.

All I knew was that they were coming into Hoboken, so I got on a subway and went down to Hoboken. And I couldn't get into the navy yard. They wouldn't let me in; I had no pass or anything. I was by this time in such a state that I was weeping bitterly, and they took me into an office. Finally somebody came along and said, "There is a group of aviators coming in. They'll be at such and such." So they sent me up there. So all I could do when they came in was cry.

Q: What was his reaction?

---

*In May 1919, three NC flying boats, including NC-1 piloted by Lieutenant Mitscher, left NAS Rockaway, New York, in an attempt to make the first transatlantic flight. Only NC-4, under the command of Lieutenant Commander Albert C. Read, USN, made it all the way to Lisbon.

Mrs. Mitscher: Just very stoic. We just got in the car and went to the apartment.

Q: Did he ever make any display of his affection?

Mrs. Mitscher: No, not in public he wouldn't.

Q: Did he have any apprehension about the flight?

Mrs. Mitscher: I'm sure he never did, no. If he did, he didn't mention it to me.

Q: You said that he was scheduled to go on the Akron?

Mrs. Mitscher: Yes, he was. There had been a lot of trouble with the lighter than air for quite some time. He had had a letter from the commanding officer wanting him to come aboard, because he felt that everything was all right with them now. So time went on. Then Commander Cecil was invited to go, too, and Admiral Moffett, and a lot of other people.*

The morning they were to go, Admiral Moffett's aide was on leave and meeting his mother coming in from New York. Admiral Cook, then captain and chief of the bureau, said that both Commander Cecil and my husband could not go on the Akron because

---
*Rear Admiral William A. Moffett, USN, Chief of the Bureau of Aeronautics from 1921 to 1933.

he had to have them there.* They were going up to Congress for something.

Admiral Moffett said, "Then I'll take Commander Cecil as my aide and Mitscher can stay here." And that's the reason why he wasn't on the Akron.

Q: That was fortunate, wasn't it? Did you ever hear him discuss Pearl Harbor? Where was he then?

Mrs. Mitscher: We were at Norfolk. The Hornet was going out; it had just been completed. We had been on the golf course with Commander and Mrs. Henderson, and we played golf.** We came into the club and were having lunch, when a bluejacket came with the message of the bombing of Pearl Harbor.

Q: What was the admiral's reaction?

Mrs. Mitscher: He was very quiet, and left to go to the ship immediately, both he and Commander Henderson. Then, of course, the Hornet was in very little after that. They went out on their trial run and then came back. They went on out and I came up here.

---

*Captain Arthur B. Cook, USN, who was assistant chief of the Bureau of Aeronautics in April 1933 and Chief from 1936 to 1939.
**Commander George R. Henderson, USN.

Q: Do you remember any comments he made?

Mrs. Mitscher: Under stress he would smile in a peculiar sort of way. The minute he read the message, I knew something had happened. Nobody else would know that, but I could tell that something had happened. He kept everything within himself. He couldn't show emotion in any way in my knowledge of him.

Q: How did you know that he loved you?

Mrs. Mitscher: I just knew. He was perfectly willing to tell me he loved me, but I doubt if he would have told anybody else he did. I always knew that he did whether he told me or not. Of course, there were many ways that he showed that he cared for me, but they're intangible.

Q: Did he make you feel cared for, well taken care of, warm when he was around?

Mrs. Mitscher: Very much so.

Q: Did he ever describe the time when Doolittle took off for the bombing of Japan?* Did you ever hear him comment on it?

Mrs. Mitscher: It was so long before he came home after that that he didn't. If we had been able to be together, eventually I'm sure he would have, but the time we were together was so short and he was so busy and there were so many people pressed in on us. If time had gone on and we'd been together, I'm sure he would have talked to me a lot about it.

Q: Actually, you were together a very little while before his death, and he was gone a great deal of that time, too.

Mrs. Mitscher: Yes. Even the time we were in Washington I knew he needed to rest. And then we went out an awful lot. He was away a lot on these speaking tours.

Q: Was he a great letter writer?

Mrs. Mitscher: Not during the last war; always before that he had been. He wrote very amusing letters to me. Of course, the First World War he was out such a short time. During the Second World War, he wrote frequently, but just a few lines at a time.

---

*On the morning of 18 April 1942, 16 B-25 bombers, with Lieutenant Colonel James H. Doolittle, USA, in the lead, took off from the Hornet (CV-8) for a daring air attack on the Japanese mainland. Of 82 crew members involved in the raid, 70 eventually returned home. Though the raid was of only marginal military impact, its greatest contribution was to U.S. morale.

Which I could understand; he was too busy. He would write that he was well and everything of that sort. A lot of the time he couldn't say where he was, until he was with the Task Force 58 when he was with the fleet.

He went from Honolulu to Espiritu Santo for a while. He wrote a little more from there, but nothing specific that would be of interest. He moved around quite a bit. He wrote frequently, but just to let us know that he was all right.

Q: In early '44 when he became the task group commander, that was a rather new concept in warfare.* Did you ever hear him make any comments on that, how successful it was, or whether he was satisfied or pleased with it?

Mrs. Mitscher: He could never stop praising the fliers in what they did. He did talk about them quite a bit. He believed that it was successful. Again, I have to say he didn't do very much talking about it at all.

Q: When he turned on the lights, after the famous Battle of the Philippine Sea, for the returning aviators--did he ever talk about that at all with you?

Mrs. Mitscher: No, and when people mentioned it to him, it

---

*Mitscher served as Commander Task Force 58, built around the fast carriers.

always seemed to embarrass him a little bit. He always said, "Well, it was nothing." No, he didn't talk about it.

Q: Do you think he liked people?

Mrs. Mitscher: Oh, yes, I do think he liked people very much.

Q: Was he a man who had close men friends?

Mrs. Mitscher: I think he had a great many. It always seemed to me that there was something that just drew men to him. For instance, lots of men, some that were not regular naval officers, in Washington, it always seemed to me that he had a great gift of having friends, their loyalty to him.

Q: You spoke of him being so concerned over losing young boys. How did he demonstrate that?

Mrs. Mitscher: He talked about that quite a bit. There is one thing that Mr. Read from New York wrote me about the other day—about the men landing on the ship when the lights were turned on. One flier they waved off, not to come aboard, but he came aboard anyway. He hit some planes they hadn't been able to get off the deck yet and killed several fliers. He went up to the admiral and told him that his brakes, or something, didn't work. The admiral said to him very gently, "You always could have gone in the drink." I assume he would have been picked up if he had gone down in the water; instead he killed several people.*

Q: You have a marvelous picture of him by Steichen.** You were told that was taken at that time?

Mrs. Mitscher: While he was waiting for those fliers to come back, I was told that. Mr. Steichen didn't tell me, although I met him one time. He had an exhibit of the war pictures in Washington, and we were both there. The officer who gave me that copy told me that at the time, so I assume that's right. I don't know for sure, but I think so. It's marvelous, I think.

Q: Have you seen him look that way frequently?

Mrs. Mitscher: Yes.

Q: I wanted to ask you about any letters. Do you have anything that you would want to have the Institute preserve for you?

---

*This incident took place in the Lexington (CV-16) after the first Battle of the Philippine Sea in June 1944. Vice Admiral Mitscher was serving as Commander Fast Carrier Task Force in the Central Pacific at the time.
**Lieutenant Commander Edward J. Steichen, USNR, a world-famous photographer who offered his services to the U.S. Navy in 1942 at age 62, and set up the Naval Aviation Photographic Unit, documenting the activities aboard aircraft carriers at the behest of Rear Admiral Arthur Radford, USN.

Mrs. Mitscher: I kept a few letters, but I would have to go over them again. They are purely personal letters.

Q: But sometimes the personal things a man says and the stories he tells are . . .

Mrs. Mitscher: There was one thing I ran across the other day that I thought you might be interested in. He came in here a couple of times and he made a speech in San Diego, and this is a copy of that speech. It said it was a copy before he made the speech. Whether they said that because maybe he might have changed some of the things he said, but it was a speech that he made while he was in here during the war, while the war was going on.

If you'd be interested in that, I will collect that. That is not too long. I will get these things together. I got them all out, there are drawers full of them, and came across a lot of things. There are many magazine articles. Then I have a few things that I had to have copies made of, because I thought they might like them at Annapolis. I have two or three of these, I'll have to straighten them out. You can read those, and see if you want them.

Q: You said that the admiral in his wallet at the time of his death had a letter that you had written him.

Mrs. Mitscher: Yes, it was written not too long before he came home. He seemed to me, in those last letters, that he was worrying very much about leaving me alone so much. It was preying on his mind a little bit, and then this letter was in answer from me about that. He apparently had carried it with him.

Q: That had been then quite a while that he had carried that letter. You meant when he was still out in the Pacific you wrote it to him?

Mrs. Mitscher: Not too long. Yes, just shortly before he came home.

Q: That would have been '45, so he would have had to have carried it for more than a year in his wallet. Did you know he had it?

Mrs. Mitscher: No.

Q: Did he ever discuss with you what he thought the Navy's position was in world affairs?

Mrs. Mitscher: No, I couldn't say that he discussed it with me. Of course, he believed in the fleet and thought it was the greatest in the world, and all of that sort of thing that he did believe in.

Q: Why did he wear that baseball cap?

Mrs. Mitscher: Only because it shaded his eyes. It wasn't a baseball cap really. They made it aboard ship for him. They seemed to make a great deal over the fact that he sat with his back so he was facing the flight deck all the time when the fliers came in. I think they had some in the athletic department, but they made that one. It had a different crown, because he couldn't keep his cap on his head out there, and he wanted something that would shade his eyes.

When the Navy painted his portrait, I was furious with him and his aide, too, because all the baseball teams had sent him caps and they didn't have the right cap there at the time.* But they could have gotten one. It had a different crown, so he had a baseball cap on. He did nothing about it and neither did the aide. I asked the artist if he could do anything about it and he said, "No."

Q: Did he have trouble with his eyes, or was it just that he wanted to be able to see better?

---
*Mitscher's portrait was painted by Lieutenant Commander Albert K. Murray, USNR.

Mrs. Mitscher: He wanted the sun out of his eyes, and it would stay on his head, which a regular cap wouldn't do sitting out there on the bridge where he sat watching the planes come in on the flight deck.

Q: Did you have any ideas when you knew him as a young man that he would be a famous personage? Sometimes one has a feeling of greatness about a person.

Mrs. Mitscher: No, I really couldn't have; that would have been impossible. Do you think you would have at that age?

Q: No, I suppose at 18 I was like any 18-year-old. At the time he became an aviator, his seriousness or his steadfastness and dedication to a principle might have made you . . .

Mrs. Mitscher: I believed in all of that. I believed he was that type of person. But that he would ever become what he was or that we would go into war, I didn't look that far ahead.

Q: The book is well-named.*

Mrs. Mitscher: Yes. I wondered about the title until I later

---

*Admiral Mitscher's biography, written by Theodore Taylor, is entitled The Magnificent Mitscher (New York: W.W. Norton & Company, Inc., 1954).

read an article that was titled "Mitscher's Magnificent Mistake." Of course, it was not a mistake in the story. It was quite an interesting article. I have it and will find it. So I have it in my mind that that's why the author named the book what he did. He must have read that article, too, because, of course, he was reading everything.

Q: Was he a profane man?

Mrs. Mitscher: Not as I knew him. In articles about him they often speak of it, but I did not think so.

Q: Was he kind to his junior officers, or would you have any way of knowing that?

Mrs. Mitscher: I suppose like anybody else, some people didn't like him, but most of them seemed to.

Interview Number 2 with Mrs. Frances Smalley Mitscher
Place: Mrs. Mitscher's home in Coronado, California
Date: 24 January 1971
Subject: Admiral Marc A. Mitscher, U.S. Navy
Interviewer: Commander Etta-Belle Kitchen, U.S. Navy (Retired)

Q: I want to take a little different approach this morning and talk something about you. I'd like you to tell me your background, and a little bit of family, because you come through so nicely on the tape. Your birthdate, place, and parents.

Mrs. Mitscher: I was born in Tacoma, Washington. My father was born in Illinois and went to the University of Illinois, and then went to law school. Then he went to Abilene, Kansas, where my mother lived. She was not born there. Her mother and father came there after the Civil War. He met my mother and they were married when she was 18 years old and he was 26, I believe.

He had a roommate in college that had moved out to Tacoma, so he came there. I was born there, and my two older sisters were born in Kansas. I grew up there. My father was an attorney. There were three girls in the family.

We were married January 16, 1913.

Q: Do you, in thinking back on your life with the admiral, have any highlight in your relationship that you can think of? Something that stands out as a particularly wonderful experience that you had with him?

Mrs. Mitscher: I can't think of anything particularly; it seemed to me I had many. But to think of some particular thing that would be of interest, I don't seem to think of anything at the moment.

Q: Maybe a period of your life that was unusually happy with him.

Mrs. Mitscher: It all seemed to be very happy after we once got together. I know I enjoyed my life in Washington very much during the period when he was a commander and until the war came and we had to leave. That was a particularly happy social time of our lives. All during that period of time we seemed to be very close, very much in love with each other, and we had a happy, pleasant life.

I didn't have too much health until I was 40. Along around there I had pneumonia, which I had two or three times before. After then, I had perfectly good health from then on.

Q: You told me, I think, last evening that you'd had T.B. as a child?*

Mrs. Mitscher: Yes. After he came back from the transatlantic flight, I got that awful flu that came through the war. Then I had another bad two years, where I was in bed six months. It was about two years before I could lead a really normal life again. I've been perfectly well ever since then.

Q: Did the admiral have a close man friend after Commander Cecil's death?**

Mrs. Mitscher: They were classmates, and they were very close friends. There was Kenneth Whiting, who was one of the early aviators--they were very close.*** He died right at the beginning of the war, he got a terrific germ of some sort and died.****

The men closely associated with him--I don't think of any other person. He had close relationships with many men that, of course, I didn't know very much about.

---

*T.B.--tuberculosis.
**Commander Henry B. Cecil, USN, was killed in the crash of the rigid airship Akron (ZRS-4) off the New Jersey coast on 4 April 1933.
***Captain Kenneth Whiting, USN, Naval Aviator #16.
****Captain Whiting had been placed on the retired list in June 1940, but was recalled to active duty after the Pearl Harbor attack as the commanding officer of the New York Naval Air Station and district aviation officer, Third Naval District. He died on 24 April 1943 from septicemia.

Q: We had a few topics to mention that I want to recall to you. As an incident of his sensitivity or kindness, in the early days of his courtship and his relationship with your mother . . .

Mrs. Mitscher: I think I told you that my mother was very much upset over my sudden marriage, and my leaving home with a naval officer whom she did not know anything about.

During that one week I went to a luncheon that someone gave me, and he asked me to make an appointment with my mother, that he would like to spend that afternoon with her talking to her, which he did. He told me that she tried to persuade him to put the marriage off to some later date, and that he did not wish to do that.

Q: But it was his idea that she might feel better if he talked to her.

Mrs. Mitscher: He wanted to talk to her, and I'm sure he hoped to explain to her or make her feel that it was all right.

Q: You told me that he sent you flowers frequently?

Mrs. Mitscher: Every day of that month that he was up there, yes, always something to wear and some for the house, most of the time both.

The woman who had the florist shop that we all knew so well, every day he got them there. She told a friend of my mother's that she didn't see why if she looked into that boy's face she would know that I was perfectly safe.

Q: Do you think that he would ever have written his biography had he lived longer?

Mrs. Mitscher: He said he would not, but, of course, I don't know. If he'd been retired and not had much to do, he might have, but I doubt it.

Q: Did he ever make any notes that you are aware of with an idea of making a record of his career?

Mrs. Mitscher: Of course, I gave a great deal to the Library of Congress. They wanted papers and all sorts of things.

But his office was bombed, and I think almost everything then was burned in his office, when he was aboard ship. That last bombing was toward the end, when, I think, there were 17 of his staff killed and he was on the bridge.*

---

*On 11 May 1945, Vice Admiral Mitscher's Task Force 58 flagship, USS Bunker Hill (CV-17) was attacked by two kamikazes. Mitscher and his remaining staff (13 were killed in the attack) were transferred to the Enterprise (CV-6), from which they were again transferred three days later when that carrier was damaged by a suicide plane.

There was tremendous mail when he was home for a week. I was staying at the Coronado Hotel, and it would stack up on the floor. All that mail was burned, so I didn't have that to give to the Library of Congress.

I had to find what was here. They seemed very pleased with what they had. I took a suitcase full of things. Then I said, "Of course, I have hundreds of letters written after his death, but I didn't think you'd want them."

And they said, "Yes, very much, because in research the people would be able to get the character of the man through the letters which they couldn't get any other way." So I chose the ones that I thought were of importance, and they have those.

Q: You also indicated that you would like to be able to impart your concept of him as a sensitive man.

Mrs. Mitscher: Yes, I would like to be able to, but I doubt if I could. That again is one of those things that I think is difficult to define. I think any friends who knew him very closely, especially my women friends, were able to see that in him. I don't know whether the men did or not.

Q: Was he at ease with women? Did he enjoy being in the company of women when he had the opportunity?

Mrs. Mitscher: He liked very much our close friends, women that we knew he liked very much and was very fond of them.

Q: When people came to your apartment or your home, how would he greet them?

Mrs. Mitscher: I think that all goes into the fact that I said he was a very good host and made his guests feel very comfortable. Most of the time they were close friends. He was very friendly to them, he was very fond of them. He was very fond of Mrs. Murray, who was Mrs. Mustin first. Of our close friends he was very fond, and very fond of my niece Betty. He liked women. I couldn't picture him ever as a flirtatious man.

Q: We spoke also of his height, as featured during the war years. They speak of him as being almost wispy.

Mrs. Mitscher: He became very small during the war, he lost so much weight. Of course, he had that very, very white skin that, in his type of life, lined it that much more. They did use the word "wispy" so much. It seems to be in the newspaper they are creating a vision or a character or something that I didn't always agree with. He was 5'9" to 5'9-1/2", and did not appear to be a particularly small man, until he lost so much weight during the war. Then he seemed much smaller. Of course, they were big ships he was on, on the bridge and all. He was very, very thin when he came home. He had absolutely no flesh on him at all, just his bones really. And as we get older we get shorter and smaller, I suppose, and this he did. That's why I showed you that little picture. He wasn't an extremely small man when he was a young man.

Q: The picture you showed me is a snapshot. I wonder what year that was taken.

Mrs. Mitscher: That was at the very beginning of the war, when he was in Honolulu, before he went on to Guam, in '42.

Q: He looks there of completely normal stature and size man, so the war certainly changed him to just hardly recognizable. I do hope that at some time the Institute might have that picture, because it does make the distinction. I think it's nice to see him in that aspect, as well as the end of the war four or five years later.

I wanted to make some reference to notes that I have made on Admiral Mitscher, taken from publications, and see if you might be able to amplify them. In his early days in the Academy when there was a story written in the books about hazing and investigation that took place, do you think that those stories, as told, for example, in the book by Taylor, are an accurate reflection of what happened?*

Mrs. Mitscher: I suppose he must have gotten his information from some place. Marc never did tell me that he took any active part in that hazing, although he was there and witnessed it. So that's all I really know about it. I don't remember in Taylor's book whether he said that he was discharged from the Navy or not--in one article it says that he was. But he told me that it got down to the last two of them, and I can't remember the other midshipman's name, but they did discharge him from the Navy, but they did not discharge Marc. I think this is very characteristic of him--that he felt that he should have been, too, then, so he resigned. And the next day his father had him reappointed. This is as I knew the story.

Q: One of the articles speaks of the incident being for drinking and another speaks of it for smoking.**

---

*In his book, The Magnificent Mitscher (New York: W.W. Norton & Company, 1954), biographer Theodore Taylor says that Mitscher joined freely in hazing as a second year midshipman, and was punished along with 200 classmates after a class fight in 1905 resulted in the death of one midshipman. He was forced to resign from the Academy "for academic reasons," but his father pulled political strings to get him reappointed. This was accomplished, but Mitscher was forced to repeat his first two years, causing him to graduate in 1910 instead of 1908 with the rest of his original class.

**In 1907, unrelated to his 1905 dismissal for hazing, Mitscher had a run-in with Academy commandant Captain William S. Benson, USN, when he was accused of drinking in his Bancroft Hall room. Mitscher stood firmly in his position that he had not been drinking, even though Benson piled on 100 demerits for gross disrespect when he would not change the story. Eventually the alcohol charge was cleared from his record. This incident is covered on pages 23-24 of Taylor's biography of Mitscher.

Mrs. Mitscher: He told me it was for smoking.

Q: Did you ever hear him sound bitter about it? It would seem not.

Mrs. Mitscher: No.

Q: One time he was with a group of boys that got themselves tattooed.

Mrs. Mitscher: Oh, yes. His classmate Underwood--they both had the same tattoo on their arms.* That was just part of it. They had a buzzard dripping blood.

Q: Did that ever cause him any embarrassment as he became older? You don't recall his making any particular reference to it?

Mrs. Mitscher: No. I think he didn't care much about it, probably thought it would have been better if he hadn't done it.

This was sent to me by--I think it was Mrs. Murray, I'm not sure. It's a perfect description of Marc--both strong and

---

*According to Taylor, midshipmen Mitscher, Herbert "Judge" Underwood, and 11 others tattooed their upper right arms during the summer of 1908 to "cement the common misery" they shared when they were among 44 midshipmen put off the USS Olympia during a summer cruise due to overcrowding and relegated back to Annapolis to join the lowly plebes on their dull cruises in local waters.

gentle, winsome and severe, shy and self-assured, boyish yet prematurely old.

Q: Had she found that description someplace?

Mrs. Mitscher: I don't know. I've got a great many of these things, I can't remember where they came from.

This is something which was sent to me which I think is interesting, and I don't know from whom. It says, "God and a soldier we adore, in time of danger, not before. The danger passes and all things righted, God is forgotten and the soldier slighted."

This is something I was very interested in, because it's a description of when a man comes home from the war--the impossibility of understanding. I just copied it out of a novel.

Q: I wanted to refer to the incident when he calmed an interruption in the interurban between Los Angeles and San Pedro one night, when he was riding with Admiral Claude Gillette.[*] That was before you were married. Do you remember his story about that?

Mrs. Mitscher: He had told me about the incident. Yes, that was before we were married. He just said that everybody got off the

---
[*]Ensign Claude S. Gillette, USN.

train rooting for him, calling him "Whitey." That's the only thing he told me about it.

Q: Because some girl was being pestered?

Mrs. Mitscher: Yes, he said the girl began to cry.*

Q: Did he like you to select his clothes?

Mrs. Mitscher: I selected them because I couldn't get him to go to the tailor. I never had anything to do with his uniforms; this was merely for civilian clothes. So I would go to the tailor and get him to telephone him and make him come to make the selection, so that he would go finally. I had a man come to the house that made his shirts and things like that. I got to know just what shoes to order for him. As far as his uniforms were concerned, I did nothing about that.

Q: Did he like to handle money? Did all of that come to you as a responsibility?

Mrs. Mitscher: No, he couldn't be bothered. It was a rare occasion to get him to write a check. He riddled my pocketbook, instead of the other way around. No, he couldn't be bothered

---

*An account of Mitscher's chivalrous action can be found on page 32 of Theodore Taylor's book.

with money. It didn't interest him really.

Q: He had, I guess in those days, a certain type of security being in the Navy.

Mrs. Mitscher: Of course, life was very different then. They got very little money when he was an ensign, but we didn't require as much in any way in those days as you do today.

Q: You just said something that I thought was very nice. I'd like to have you repeat it. You said, "I read many things about him . . ."

Mrs. Mitscher: And I wouldn't recognize the man as I knew him, that they have written about. So I feel that there were two sides to the man, one that someone else knew, and I didn't know that side of him.

Q: You said something that was interesting, too, that newspapers use words that maybe are appropriate and maybe they aren't. That's why we're talking to you, to get your view of him as a man.

Mrs. Mitscher: I had said that sometimes I didn't recognize him in some of the things that were written, and the man or officer would seem a little bit astonished at that. But he being the character that he was, which to me, as I'd gone through life, was quite different and quite unusual. I knew a different side of a man that they knew as a war commander.

Q: And that all is part of the man. You spoke of knowing Ken Whiting, when you were down at Pensacola.* Could you give me a few comments as to your recollections?

Mrs. Mitscher: He was in this very small group of aviators, so all through our life we were close friends. My husband was the air officer when the Saratoga was first commissioned, then he was the executive officer when Captain Whiting was the commanding officer. There was a close association. They were in the Navy Department together, and all through our life. He died very shortly after World War II started. They were on duty in Washington, and died then.

Q: How do you remember him?

Mrs. Mitscher: He was a very lovable character, and a very loyal and wonderful friend. He was quite unusual in a way that I can't very well describe.

---

*Lieutenant Kenneth Whiting, USN, Naval Aviator #16.

Q: He has been written about, but I'm sure not nearly as much as would be if he were alive in modern days.

Mrs. Mitscher: Ken Whiting was a very lovable man, and I'm sure a very fine officer, very colorful.

Q: What did the admiral think about you flying?

Mrs. Mitscher: He didn't want me to fly very much. On one of my flying trips, when we left Calcutta for Agra, it was an old DC-3 that to us looked like it was tied together with string, very crowded, seats close together. There was an American man aboard that showed that he was not very calm, very frightened. I leaned over to Mrs. Jones and I said, "You know, Marc wouldn't let me fly," and we had a good hard laugh that we were in this old plane.

When he came home, he didn't think that civilian flying had settled down enough after the war, and he did not want me to fly. This was in 1945, when he was going on these trips around.

Q: One time you threatened to go up in a blimp.

Mrs. Mitscher: I wanted to go, and he wouldn't let me. That was on Montauk Point, when we was right there at the beginning of World War I. Then it turned up on end, so I was very glad I wasn't in it.

Q: You saw the name Luis de Flores and you said that reminded you of a story.*

Mrs. Mitscher: Luis de Flores told me this after Marc's death. He was out there on the ship with him as a guest during the war. It was probably a kamikaze that came down, and it was coming right toward the bridge. He was part Spanish and very excitable. He kept saying, "Why doesn't he shoot? Why doesn't he shoot?"

Then Marc said, "Sh, he might hear you." He came right over the bridge and went down into the water. They never knew whether he was dead or committing suicide.

Q: Did you hear the admiral speak about his great loss of the squadron at Midway?**

Mrs. Mitscher: Yes, I did. He talked about that quite a bit, when he came in temporarily to Coronado. We didn't have much time together, but he talked a lot about it. I seemed to feel

---
*Rear Admiral Luis de Flores, USNR.
**As a captain, Mitscher commanded the carrier Hornet (CV-8) from October 1941 until July 1942, a period including both the Doolittle Raid (April 1942) and the Battle of Midway (June 1942). During the latter action, Torpedo Squadron 8, launched from the Hornet, was virtually obliterated. Of 30 pilots and crew members sent up in 15 planes, only one person, Ensign George H. Gay, USNR, survived.

that they all flew and gave their lives, knowing that they were, to try to do what they were supposed to do. That was my impression. And I know that he felt a great love and feeling for that squadron, and I think he tried to do certain things about them afterwards.

Q: Maybe he tried to get them the Medal of Honor, and they eventually were awarded the Navy Cross.

Mrs. Mitscher: Yes, he felt that they should have had the Medal of Honor, I'm sure of that.

Q: I have a reference here to a time when the admiral came back after the Solomons. He made a trip home and he was ill. My reference is that at that time he did put his arms around you in public.

Mrs. Mitscher: Yes, that was the first time he came home. When he came in, I guess he couldn't very well help himself, I was there, yes. But I knew that he didn't want very much of a demonstration from me. He looked so badly that I was quite shocked at the time, but he was all right when he had a month's rest.

Q: What was his highest weight? I saw a picture that you had where he had a little bit of fullness in his cheeks.

Mrs. Mitscher: That was when he was 35 years old in Washington. That was the only time we had that much shore duty, we had three years at that time. He didn't like it. He usually weighed around 135-140 pounds.

Q: When he came back after the Solomons, he was down to 115 pounds.

Mrs. Mitscher: I guess that must have been right. But I'm not surprised because there really was no flesh on him at all.

Q: Did you ever know his parents?

Mrs. Mitscher: Oh, yes. They came out here one time and spent a year or a year and a half here with us. They were with us for a while here in Coronado. His father was anxious to leave Oklahoma, but I think his mother was too homesick and they went back there. Of course, we visited them in their home in Oklahoma City twice--once not too long after we were married, and as we crossed the continent we stopped there.

Q: Admiral Mitscher is quoted in a number of places as to his very deep hate of the Japanese. Do you think those are true reflections of his feelings?

Mrs. Mitscher: The newspapers, it seems, do dwell on that a little bit, in a way that makes a picture of him that isn't quite right. I've always felt that in fighting a war like that, they had to hate them in order to be able to do it at all, in his own mind. That is something that I know about him that the newspaper man wouldn't feel. They do make quite a bit of that. In a speech he made, it's how he does feel. That is part of what I mean that I know of his sensitiveness. I know that he had to make himself hate them in order to fight, and he fought because that was his job. But I've always felt that they make him sound a little bad along those lines, but maybe not. When you read that speech, you'll hear what he has to say himself about it.

Q: I would assume that when you see your best friends killed and your young men being killed, it might not be so difficult to hate.

Mrs. Mitscher: No, then, too, after Pearl Harbor he would feel that way, I'm sure.

Q: We are going to try to find the exact wording of the letter which was in the admiral's wallet at the time of his death. But you do recall generally what you said, and I'd like to have it in your own words.

Mrs. Mitscher: I wrote to him that in his last few letters he sounded as if he were very worried and it was bothering him that he had left me alone for so long.

"Please know, dear, that I know only happiness for you that you are doing what you lived your life for." That's as much as I can remember of it.

Q: I can understand why he did preserve it, and keep it with him. It must have given him a great deal of comfort. But he didn't refer to it? You didn't know that he had kept it?

Mrs. Mitscher: No.

Q: I think that your words and the description of the man in your relationships as he was with you will be a truly valuable experience for the Institute.

Mrs. Mitscher: I was very much afraid I might sound too sentimental and too wifely, making much more of it than I should, because he would not have liked that very much.

Q: Well, who knows? But you can only say how he seemed to you, which is what we're talking about. Not thinking about what someone thinks you should have said, or even what he would want you to say, although that's all a part of your love and affection for him, not to do something to displease him.

Interview Number 1 with Mrs. Mary Smith

Place: Annapolis, Maryland

Date: 24 March 1978

Subject: Biography

Interviewer: John T. Mason, Jr.

Q: Mrs. Smith, I've been looking forward to this conversation with you. Would you tell me about your father, who was in the Navy?*

Mrs. Smith: Pa was a captain in the Professors' Corps, and Roy said, "How did he get to be captain?"**

I said, "I haven't the faintest idea." But I know he was one, because in those days, he wore a uniform at the Naval Academy all the time. And in all of the pictures of him, he had captain's stripes, and he certainly didn't make them up.

---
*Mrs. Smith's father was Philip R. Alger, who was born 29 September 1859 and died 23 February 1912. He was the top man in the class when he was graduated from the Naval Academy in 1880 and went on to become perhaps the foremost ordnance expert in the Navy in the closing years of the 19th century. As such, he was more valuable to the service on duty at the Bureau of Ordnance in Washington than by continuing the usual sea-shore rotation of a line officer. Thus, he became a Professor of Mathematics in 1890. The Professors of Mathematics were a small group of officers who constituted essentially a separate corps within the Navy of the time. Alger was a prolific writer, often published in the Proceedings, and served as secretary and treasurer of the Naval Institute from 1903 to the time of his death. For more on his career, see Rear Admiral Austin M. Knight, USN, "Professor Philip Rounseville Alger, U.S. Navy: An Appreciation," U.S. Naval Institute Proceedings, March 1912, pages 1-5.

**Alger was promoted to the rank of captain in the Professors of Mathematics in the year 1905. The Roy referred to here is Mrs. Smith's son, Captain Roy C. Smith III, USNR(Ret.).

Navy Wives - 65
Smith #1 - 2

Q: What was the Professors' Corps?

Mrs. Smith: Well, Paul Dashiell was in it, I think. Paul Dashiell was way before your time, I'm sure.*

Q: Yes.

Mrs. Smith: I really don't know. I really haven't any idea. One takes it for granted. Did you ever ask exactly what your father did? Did you ever ask him?

Q: It had something to do with teaching, didn't it?

Mrs. Smith: Oh, yes, definitely. It was mathematics. He was head of the department of mechanics.** And we lived in a double house, a house this way, and a house going that way, with Professor Hendrickson, who was mathematics.***

Q: And this was what date approximately?

---

*Paul J. Dashiell, who taught at the Naval Academy from 1892 to 1932, eventually reached the rank of captain as a Professor of Mathematics. Dashiell was chairman of the intercollegiate football rules committee, 1894-1911, and Naval Academy football head coach, 1904-1906; he was known as "father of Naval Academy athletics."
**The academic departments of mechanics and mathematics were combined around 1907. Alger was a department head until the merger.
***Professor William W. Hendrickson, who was in the Naval Academy class of 1863 and resigned as a lieutenant commander in 1873. He was part of the Academy faculty at the time and remained in that capacity after his resignation. By the turn of the century, he was head of the department of mathematics.

Mrs. Smith: This must have been 1899, must have been 1900.

Q: Around the turn of the century.

Mrs. Smith: Yes, because I tell you, I remember so well the family saying how strange it is and all this stuff. And then on the far corner was Professor Terry, but he was what they called "skinny" in those days--physics.* I don't think he had anything to do with the Academy as a past. And I don't think Hendrickson did either. I don't know where they came from. They were just there, as far as I was concerned. Then the other half of our house was Halsey, Bill Halsey's father, and then, of course, the paymaster, the doctor, and so on like that.**

Q: How many midshipmen were there in those days? How big a place was it?

Mrs. Smith: Oh, I would think only a few hundred, because they used to come out, for instance, and form and drill on the area around the Herndon Monument.*** Or have they moved the Herndon

---
*Professor Nathaniel M. Terry, who became an instructor in the department of physics and chemistry in 1873 and served as head of the department from 1886 onward.
**Lieutenant Commander William F. Halsey, USN, whose son, William F. Halsey, Jr., was a fleet commander during World War II and one of the Navy's few five-star admirals.
***The monument, which still stands across the street from the Naval Academy chapel, commemorates William Lewis Herndon, a Navy explorer of the 19th century. While in command of a ship named Central America in 1857, Herndon sacrificed his life to save the lives of passengers and crew during a storm off Cape Hatteras.

Monument? The Herndon Monument is a shaft, used to be right in front of the chapel. The works used to come out and drill around there. And around that time, they were finishing what was known as Oklahoma, which is the area in front of Rodgers and Upshur Road.* Rogers was new houses, and that got to be the drilling area, but there weren't very many midshipmen then. There couldn't have been. There couldn't have been. And I remember the night that they won the Army-Navy game, and the class of 1907 was carrying on, you know. And, of course, we all oozed out of the houses for that. And that was the time that Zimmerman wrote "Anchor's Aweigh," and it was produced the first time that night, or that day, whatever it was.**

Q: Where was that game played in those days?

Mrs. Smith: Oh, in Philadelphia, always.

Q: Always in Philadelphia.

---

*The nickname Oklahoma was chosen by midshipmen for what was officially named Worden Field (the parade grounds) because like the western territory petitioning for statehood at the time, it was out in the middle of nowhere. Rodgers and Upshur roads, which bound two of the sides of Worden Field, are lined with quarters for senior officers on the faculty and staff.

**Naval Academy bandmaster Charles Zimmerman made it a practice to compose a march in honor of each graduating class. Midshipman Alfred Hart Miles, class of 1907, wrote words to accompany Zimmerman's music, and the result was "Anchor's Aweigh."

Mrs. Smith: Always in Philadelphia.* Everybody went to Philadelphia. It was lovely. They had a train come in. Everybody got on the train, you know, when I got old enough to go, and you took a picnic lunch and you went up, and the train stopped not far from the field. Everybody went to the game, came back, came home. Can you think of anything neater?

Q: You must have had a very gay time on that train coming back, especially . . .

Mrs. Smith: No, Sir, in those days nobody drank. Nobody drank anything.

Q: Nobody drank?

Mrs. Smith: No. My father always had a whiskey and soda when he read a book in the evening, and he had claret for dinner. And if they had a dinner party, they had a cocktail first and wine. No, nobody drank. Nobody began drinking until the Volstead Act.** I mean it. That was what--you can't legislate people doing things, and now they are trying to legislate God knows what, like

---

*Though usually played in Philadelphia, the Army-Navy series, that started in 1890 with a Navy victory, has also been played at West Point, Annapolis, Princeton, Chicago, Baltimore, and Pasadena, California.
**The Volstead Act, the prohibition enforcement act growing out of the 18th amendment to the Constitution, went into effect 17 January 1920.

marijuana. You couldn't do it.

Q: It just makes people want it all the more.

Mrs. Smith: Well, it's so easy to get. I mean, they can grow it. I read the other day that some innocent old lady was growing . . .

I don't remember when, but they were building Bancroft Hall.* They tore down Stribling Row.** I think Stribling Row approximately must have been where the boat house is, in that general area. And my father used to--they had those Old Quarters. Have they moved them? Have they got those first and second class seats, round sort of thing where you sat near the library, or have you moved them?***

Q: They're not there.

Mrs. Smith: Well, they were. There was a round sort of paved place where you could sit, you know. I mean, a round seat, as I remember it. I mean, it's just there. You don't go and look at it carefully. But my father said it was first and second class

---

*Bancroft Hall, the dormitory for midshipmen, was constructed between 1901 and 1906.
 **Stribling Row consisted of five brick dormitories which housed the midshipmen from 1853 to 1869.
 ***The first and second class benches, reserved for upperclassmen as a privilege of seniority, now face the main entrance to Bancroft Hall.

seats. The place was very small. And the entire bunch would go out and march and, of course, they were only building in the area of--Bancroft Hall was being built.

Q: The river came way up in there, didn't it?

Mrs. Smith: Well, there was all made ground, and masses of mud, you know, horrible, black, sticky mud, and they filled in--I don't remember their filling it in, but there was a canalish place in front between us, our house, and the armory.* And I remember there was a boardwalk in front. I gave Roy some old photographs the other day of the boardwalk running along in front of the houses. And there was no wall back of the houses, and one day I wasn't supposed to go down there, and there was a Mrs. Keeley, who would not give up her house. And it was approximately where the Commandant's house is, I guess--in between the Superintendent and the Commandant--a little wooden house, you know.

Q: She was a lady from the town?

Mrs. Smith: God knows who she was, probably an old crone. Anyhow, she lived there, and it was an amusement of the young to

---

*The cover of the July-August 1981 issue of *Shipmate*, the Naval Academy Alumni Association magazine, featured a montage of postcards picturing the Naval Academy shortly after the turn of the century. One of the postcards showed the "canal" between Dahlgren Hall and the double houses on Porter Road.

go and run around screaming. We didn't throw stones at her or anything like that. She wouldn't give up. Finally the law pushed her out, and the house was haunted. We used to go down, and you can imagine how you would. I wasn't supposed to. We lived up at the other end. It seemed further then than it does now.

Q: She supposedly was haunting the house?

Mrs. Smith: Yeah, sure. Evil spirits. And I snuck off one day and went down to see our new house, all by myself, and I went along, and I went out in the back yard and I sank in the mud. That's what happened. This horrible, black, sticky mud. And I sank down to my ankles, just about. I was terrified. You can imagine. And I screamed like a banshee, I'm sure, because the sentry at the gate, who could see me then--you see, I was out in the back and there were no fences, no nothing, and he dropped his gun and came roaring down and pulled me out. I had to promise not to tell on him and all that business. In those days, you knew all the watchmen. That's why Roy got in such trouble, because the old watchman said to me--you see, we were there later, after we were there on duty, my husband was--and the watchman said to me, "Of course, I knew your boy when he was growing up. So a bunch of midshipmen french out. He's the only one we recognize, so he gets the demerits." It was bad.*

---

*Mrs. Smith's son, Roy C. Smith III, had to leave the Naval Academy in the 1930s when he was a midshipman because he was caught sneaking out of the Academy grounds.

Q: The watchmen, were they Marines in those days?

Mrs. Smith: No. I don't know what corps they belonged to. They wore blue uniforms--plain blue clothes, as I remember. And the gate--well, I haven't looked at it, but the gate, I think, is the same as now.

Q: The gate on Maryland Avenue?

Mrs. Smith: I mean the gate itself, the 1907 gate, but I mean the gate houses.* Used to be plenty big for anything that went on. But then they were building, as I said, Bancroft Hall, and we had a marvelous time with that. We used to go down there and race through it, which we were not supposed to do, of course. And the watchmen were not as quick as us, and they were a little fatter. And we used to go in and they'd chase us and tell us to go out, and we would wiggle through the partitions, which were not plastered, between the rooms. We would go down here, you see, about six rooms while those poor things were coming in, down the hall. It must have been maddening.

Q: These Navy brats.

Mrs. Smith: We weren't doing any terrible harm, you know, but we

---

*The Maryland Avenue gate structure was donated to the Naval Academy in 1932 as a 25th anniversary gift from the class of 1907.

just weren't supposed to be there. And they were building the chapel, and we got into trouble with that, more or less, because I remember, for instance, they were hauling these big slabs of granite up and would have a sling around, you know. And we snuck on a couple of times and sat one of us on each side of the sling and rode up, got off and came down the scaffolding. You know, I don't know why we didn't break our necks. Of course, we were discovered doing that because we got well scolded.

Q: Did they have a football field there at that time?

Mrs. Smith: The football field was Oklahoma. You know where it is.

Q: Yes.

Mrs. Smith: And the boat houses were along there, too.

Q: Yes.

Mrs. Smith: Little funny ones down on the shore along there. That was, I think, the major reason for that big field. And it was long afterwards when they were adding and adding out in front of Bancroft Hall--they have added to Bancroft Hall since, so much that you wouldn't know it. And speaking of the mud, I remember perfectly well one day me and a couple of pals were watching—of course, we used to put our noses into everything, watch all the sports and all the things going on, you know. And on this occasion, we were sitting watching Admiral Hart all in his starchy whites. You know how starchy he always looked. And he was walking backwards in front of the awkward squad and directing them fiercely, and they were plunging along after him, you know.* In those days midshipmen were younger than now and less experienced.

Q: Now you're talking about the period of early 1930s when he was there as Superintendent?

Mrs. Smith: No. Heavens, no. He was a lieutenant.

Q: When he was a lieutenant, still. I see.

Mrs. Smith: A lieutenant. When he was Superintendent, no, we were in Newport when he was Superintendent, no.

Q: I see.

Mrs. Smith: No. He was very young and inexperienced, too. He was backing off, he had the awkward squad coming after him like this, you see, and all of a sudden he stepped in one of these

---

*Lieutenant (junior grade) Thomas C. Hart, USN, infantry drill instructor from 1902 to 1904. As a rear admiral, Hart was Superintendent of the Naval Academy from 1931 to 1934.

places like I stepped in and went down like that. And he wasn't quick, and the awkward squad was advancing, advancing, advancing. We were just screaming with mirth that they were going to mow him right down like a runaway car. But he came to in time, and stopped them right practically standing on his feet, and they had to pull him out. We thought that was hilarious.

Q: I bet he looked like a mess, didn't he?

Mrs. Smith: He did. We thought, oh, that was hilarious. He didn't think so at all.

Q: Where did you go to school?

Mrs. Smith: Well, I went to school at Green Street, here, an Annapolis school.

Q: The Green Street School.

Mrs. Smith: Sure, we all did, traipsed out there. Then eventually I went away to boarding school when I was 13 or 14.

Q: Tell me first about Annapolis itself. What was it like in those days?

Mrs. Smith: We knew very little about Annapolis, because, you see, we lived in the compound, if you understand, behind the wall.

Q: But going to school on Green Street, you must have mixed with some of the Annapolitan children.

Mrs. Smith: Oh, yes, yes, we did.

Q: And gone into their homes, did you not?

Mrs. Smith: And Mrs. Schamyl Cochran, who used to be Isabel Miller--ever know her? Well, for a long time here he had a prep school like . . .

Q: Werntz's.*

Mrs. Smith: Yes, Werntz. And this was after that. Cochran had one later. But Isabel was very pretty and was considered in those days "fast," although heaven knows she couldn't have been any age.

Q: What was being "fast"?

---

*Robert L. Werntz was graduated from the Naval Academy in 1884, resigned his commission in 1890, and later established the Werntz Preparatory School on Maryland Avenue in Annapolis. After his death in 1931 the school continued until a fire destroyed the building in 1937.

Mrs. Smith: God knows. The family told me I wasn't to speak to her, my mother did, so naturally I spoke to her, you know what I mean. But really, I remember that there was a theater on Conduit Street. I saw the first theater I'd ever been to. Eleanor Robson came and played there. And there was a movie theater on Main Street, right about opposite of where Davis used to be, and it cost five cents. We never went except with Mrs. Terry. Mrs. Terry liked to do things, and her daughter and I used to do things together. And we used to go there.

Q: You had to be chaperoned when you went to the movie?

Mrs. Smith: Well, you only went in the evenings, as I remember it. I don't know, we couldn't ever have gone to the matinee, come on.

Q: Saturday afternoon?

Mrs. Smith: No. No. I don't remember any midshipmen there. Midshipmen were never allowed out. They were only allowed out very, very short times on Saturday and Sunday; that's all. No running around in those days. And I remember when I was engaged, my mother-in-law, who was Miss Sampson once upon a time--no, I'm mixing it up.* When my daughter was engaged to Poyntell Staley--

---
*Mrs. Smith's mother-in-law was Margaret Aldrich Sampson, daughter of the Superintendent of the Naval Academy from 1886 to 1890. She married Lieutenant Roy C. Smith, Sr., in 1887.

Captain Staley, retired now, and she was a Quaker, and she said to me, "At least he didn't marry one of those horrible Annapolis crabs."* Anybody born in Annapolis is called an Annapolis crab.

Q: It's crab town, of course.

Mrs. Smith: Yes, and I said, "But he was born in Annapolis."**

"Ooh," she said, "terrible." Well, again, recovering, she said, "Well, at least he wasn't one of those people that walked around and girls went down and met them for dates."

"Well," I said, "what else could you do? They couldn't come out." We all walked down to the gate at free time and we spent our entire afternoon walking around the yard, around, around, around, you know. That's all you could do. Imagine, you wouldn't do that today, would you? Know any girls today who'd do that?

Q: I doubt it.

Mrs. Smith: No. And I remember the old gymnasium, which used to be down, round old thing, you know, where it used to be, down—it's hard to think now.*** It must be approximately at the end

---
*Lieutenant (junior grade) Poyntell C. Staley, Jr., USN.
**Poyntell Staley, Jr. was born 11 March 1910 in Altoona, Pennsylvania.
***The old gymnasium, which was originally the main building of Fort Severn where the Naval Academy was established in 1845, sat on the Severn River at Windmill Point. Fort Severn, initially slated for historic preservation, was demolished in 1909.

of the boathouse. And they had a wonderful affair one time. They had some Japanese wrestlers who came and gave an exhibit, and they were marvelous looking--great, monstrous, fat things, you know. And, of course, to us in those days, nobody went around bare, and they had very little on. We were not supposed to go. My ma was rather a stickler for proprieties, but we went, naturally. And we were fascinated, because they came out, you know how they do. They'd strut on the mat, and they advanced like this. And one went BOP! to the other one, then this one went BOP! to this one, so to speak. And you'd think they were going to splash, they were so fat. And a couple of the ladies in the front row fainted.

Q: Fainted?

Mrs. Smith: Yes, fainted. We thought that was vastly amusing. Ma didn't faint; she had better sense. I forget, not the Superintendent's wife, I don't know who they were, but anyway, they just fainted.

Q: What kind of theatricals did they put on at the Academy?

Mrs. Smith: I don't remember they had any then.

Q: They didn't?

Mrs. Smith: They may have, but I don't remember any. Up to the time when I went away to boarding school, I don't remember any. I must have been 14, 15. And then after that, I came home and stayed at home and took French and music lessons in the ancient way; you know, you don't get educated; you get finished.

Q: But you didn't have anything to do with your own age group in Annapolis?

Mrs. Smith: Yes, I did. I had two very close friends. One was Caroline Wells, who still lives here, although she seems to have retired into a home. And one was Rosalee Balk, who doesn't live here, married a naval officer. And her father, Mr. Balk, had-- there were four automobiles in town and he had one. He taught her to drive, a most advanced man. We used to go out riding in it. It had a little back tunnel thing--of course, it was open, with back steps and you stepped up to stand in the back. And you went along on the street, you know, and people would come out and yell and scream at you: "Get a horse. What do you think you're doing?" And we used to ride out West Street, which doesn't look the way it is now. It was a narrow little road out to the water works. Have the water works disappeared, or is it still there?

Q: I guess it must have disappeared.

Mrs. Smith: There used to be water works at Parole, I guess, not terribly far. The horses went plop, plop, plop, you know, not very fast. But that was one of our diversions, you might say.

Q: Did you know the Worthingtons?

Mrs. Smith: Sure. They're cousins.

Q: Oh, they're cousins of yours. Joe is a cousin of yours?*

Mrs. Smith: They're Taylor cousins. Yes, you remind me. Every time I come down there, I think I'm going to go see Margaret. I've got two Taylor cousins in Washington that I always mean to see. It's awfully difficult to manage because out here, I can't just walk around the corner. Ann has a thousand occupations. Of course, Roy's busy with his books. So it's all very well, and I arrive, and then people that I know well call up, and we do things, you know what I mean.

Q: You knew Margaret Hill, too, did you?**

Mrs. Smith: Sure, I knew Margaret Hill.

Q: She's older than you, of course.

---

*Rear Admiral Joseph M. Worthington, USN (Ret.), an Annapolis native and graduate of the Naval Academy in 1924. Admiral Worthington's oral history is in the Naval Institute collection.
**Mrs. Harry W. Hill, whose husband was Superintendent of the Naval Academy from 1950 to 1952.

Mrs. Smith: Well, not very much. And Juli, her brother, what's ever happened to him?*

Q: I guess he's dead.

Mrs. Smith: Is he dead? And then Katherine Nelson, who married Del Valle.** Is she still here?

Q: I think so.

Mrs. Smith: I haven't seen her in 10,000 years. When I come down, I'm usually here about ten days. I see Nancy Gearing, who I remember as running around, so to speak. She's younger than me. In fact, she said the other day she's 70. Hard to believe. And Caroline and Rosalee, those are my two special friends, and, of course, the Munroe girls; Emily was my contemporary. In those days, when you started going to hops, you went sort of in layers. Golda went with 1906, you see, and then her sister, Louise, who married Reifsnider, classmate of my husband's, was next, and then Emily was next.*** And each year, you know, we new ones looked at the older ones as antiques.

Q: Tell me about the hops.

---

*Julius Hall III was a non-graduate of the Naval Academy class of 1911, and died in West Virginia in March 1957.
**Lieutenant General Pedro A. Del Valle, USMC.
***Vice Admiral Lawrence F. Reifsnider, USN.

Mrs. Smith: You had a chaperone.

Q: How old were you when you went to hops?

Mrs. Smith: Oh, land!

Q: Sixteen?

Mrs. Smith: No, was I 16? I guess 16, 17, not before that. Seventeen, 18, around there. But the midshipmen were our age, you know.

Q: Yes, yes. Well, tell me about the hops.

Mrs. Smith: Well, of course, by that time, when I was going to hops, my father had been ordered--all the time he was secretary-treasurer of the Naval Institute, in addition to his other duties--you see, to go backwards a bit, we were living down on what I think of as Porter Row.

Mrs. Smith: And Mr. Roosevelt was the President and he let it be known he was the one who put in the idea of you had to have exercise fitness.* You had to either ride 100 miles or walk so many miles or, you know, be sure that you were fit. Isn't he the one that did that?

---
*Theodore Roosevelt, President from 1901 to 1909.

Q: Teddy Roosevelt? I wouldn't be surprised.

Mrs. Smith: My father decided he would rather ride 100 miles on a bicycle than walk or run. But we were there, and he, the President, decided it was ridiculous to have mechanics, so it was coalesced, mechanics and mathematics together, and Professor Stimson Brown, who is Mrs. Kalbfus's father, moved into our house, and then it was a question of whether we'd live in Washington—Pa had duty at ordnance bureau all the time—or in Annapolis, where, of course, there were five of us and school business and the Naval Institute.* Ma decided to stay in Annapolis. So then we lived in 5 Maryland Avenue, which is now quite changed in appearance.

Q: You were going to tell me about a hop, going to a hop, and how it was conducted.

Mrs. Smith: Hops, that's right. I was going to say that I don't remember that there was a reception committee but Mrs. Stuart Brown tells me, did tell me—she's now dead—that when they were there on duty, that she was one of the hop hostesses.** Maybe they had them in the background, but they weren't visible.

Q: Where were they held?

---

*Captain Stimson J. Brown, USN; Mrs. Edward C. Kalbfus.
**Mary Ann Brown (Mrs. Stuart S. Brown).

Mrs. Smith: They were held in the boathouse.

Q: In the boathouse?

Mrs. Smith: The big ones--for instance, the June ball, was in the armory, which was murder, because those blocks were put in flat on cement. I mean, it was a cement floor.

Q: You couldn't really dance very well, could you?

Mrs. Smith: It was murder on your feet, I'm telling you. And also, they had drill in there, and dropping the muskets, you know, the musket on the floor loosened all those things. I don't know what they've done with it since. They've made it a skating rink, haven't they?* But the major hops were over in the boathouse, and everybody could go except plebes, so you know the Academy wasn't too huge.

Q: What kind of music did you have?

Mrs. Smith: I guess we had the Naval Academy band. I don't remember. It must have been something like that. We certainly

---

*The armory, Dahlgren Hall, was attached to the dormitory, Bancroft Hall, and completed in 1903. In 1974 the building was converted to the midshipmen recreation center, and a skating rink and snack bar installed. Most of the Academy dances and social functions are still held here.

didn't have anything like what you have today. You had waltzes and two-steps, and I don't remember anything else, as a matter of fact.

Q: Probably those two.

Mrs. Smith: Now and then they had a thing they called the barn dance.

Q: They had barn dances, too?

Mrs. Smith: Well, I mean, the barn dance, you merely pranced down more or less like a polka.

Q: Yes.

Mrs. Smith: That sort of thing. My poor ma, I was trying to think about it. You know, it's funny, when you look back. I can remember here and here, and how I got from here to here is a complete blank. And I can't remember my poor ma--she must have walked down with us, because midshipmen couldn't ride in a carriage. We walked from 5 Maryland Avenue all the way down to the boathouse, which I would regard now as quite . . .

Q: Midshipmen couldn't come get you.

Mrs. Smith: Certainly not, or take you home either.

Q: You had to meet them there at the dance.

Mrs. Smith: Later on, I think they could take you home. Yes, because we used to have hot chocolate afterwards sometimes, but that was later. In the beginning, they didn't come out and get you, because you didn't need a chaperone going. Ma certainly must have walked down with us to be there, because I remember the old ladies--you know, you think of them as old ladies, it's your mother--sitting around in a long row of chairs like that, around a wall, and if you had no partner, you took refuge with her.

Q: Became a wallflower.

Mrs. Smith: Yes, that's where you got to be a wallflower. Thank God I never had to be a wallflower. I would have hated it!

Q: How did you arrange a date with a midshipmen if he couldn't come to call? How did you do this?

Mrs. Smith: Well, because--how did we? I don't remember their telephoning. We met them at the gate, of course, you see, and then walked with them. We went to football practice, for one thing.

Q: And that's where you saw them.

Mrs. Smith: I mean, you could. That's one of those blanks. I remember when we went there, when we left the Torpedo Station and my husband was ordered, the bank crashed in Memphis, you know, in Central America business. And my older daughter was 17, I guess, going on 18, and my younger daughter was two years younger.* And before that, I guess, because Lou was awfully young. I guess she was just 16, and we had come to the Academy. I went from Newport. I had to leave the house there, and came to Annapolis to stay with Ma and finish out the spring term of school. Then I went on down to Panama, you see, in June. And Roy, of course, had, as usual, lots of friends he was to bring out, and Ma used to feed them by dozens and thoroughly enjoy it. I mean, having eight or ten for lunch was nothing to her. She had a nice colored woman and so on. But Roy said to me, "Now, I want you to understand, Mother, my sisters are too young to go out with my friends." Very snooty. Naturally, they were looking forward to a good time. Who wouldn't? He was very starchy. So they went down one afternoon with some other girls they knew, daughters in the Yard, you know. With Navy children, you usually find somebody you knew. And they went down to football practice, and they both met some gents. And Lou came back, had been invited by Roy's company commander to the first hop. Nearly killed him! He

_____
    *Mary Alger Smith was born on 22 June 1915, her sister Louisa Taylor Smith was born on 24 April 1917.

had nothing to do with it and disapproved haughtily. You can imagine. He nearly died. He told her she couldn't do it, and she said, "Don't be silly." She said to me, "I'm scared to death. I don't know how to dance. I'm scared to death; I'm only going because of Roy's carrying on. I don't think she had a very good time, but she made the point. But in my day, there were chaperones all over the place. And we used to go sailing all the time. For weekends, we used to go sailing on the old <u>Argo</u>, and the <u>Robert Center</u>.

Q: But not with midshipmen?

Mrs. Smith: Yes, always with midshipmen.

Q: With midshipmen?

Mrs. Smith: Yes. We'd meet them at the gate and go sailing. I don't remember they came out in town. They must have come out in town.

Q: Was this on Sunday afternoon?

Mrs. Smith: Sunday afternoon, Saturday afternoon. I remember because my mother gave me a big, in those days, coming out tea, and then there was a second one on the next day, on Saturday, for midshipmen, on Saturday afternoon. But they found ways of getting hold of us if they wanted to, you know. But in those days, everybody didn't have a telephone. Nobody had a car.

Q: No. Telephones were rare.

Mrs. Smith: Life was very simple. Very simple.

Q: Tell me about your coming out party.

Mrs. Smith: Well, my coming out party--a million midshipmen, you know, and all the girls I knew. We had a grand time, but don't think we had any drinks.

Q: You served tea.

Mrs. Smith: In those days, even a long time afterwards, everybody had tea. You were invited to tea, you and your husband. Ma and Pa and all the rest of them, they had tea parties. And even when we had duty at the Torpedo Station, we went there for duty from China in 1928. Am I right? Yes. We went to China in '25, came back in '28. And then every afternoon at Torpedo Station Island, you know--now it's Goat Island--there was a band came over and played music and there was a station afternoon at home. Everybody was at home, and people would come to see you, take the ferry, but you never had anything but tea.

Q: Tea and cakes and things.

Mrs. Smith: Tea and cakes.

Q: Little sandwiches?

Mrs. Smith: Sandwiches, that's right. Nobody dreamed of having anything else. And then, of course, when we were there, Prohibition was still on on the base. You couldn't have anything to drink on the base, so if you had a dinner party, you went to some friend's house and had a drink and came back, but nobody had very many drinks.

Q: Was wine used more extensively then at dinners?

Mrs. Smith: Well, yes. I remember the dinner parties my father and mother had. There were two or three wine glasses, you know. As I remember, they had a cocktail first, I imagine one; I can't imagine any more. And then you had wine with dinner. And then afterwards, in the old-fashioned way, the ladies went in the other room and had coffee, and the gents had . . .

Q: Brandy.

Mrs. Smith: Brandy or what have you in the dining room. It was a very different life. And you had 99 courses. You know what I mean. Gosh . . .

Q: You couldn't eat everything.

Mrs. Smith: Well, the thing is, you had a little. I mean, you had soup, you had an entree, you had fish or chicken . . .

Q: For the main course.

Mrs. Smith: No, roast was the main course. And you had salad and had dessert and coffee.

Q: Was it custom, also, that at the table, at the dinner party, you changed conversation with partners when the course changed?

Mrs. Smith: You mean in a wave around?

Q: You talked to one person or the other person.

Mrs. Smith: Not in my family's house, because, as my sister says, when an Alger can't talk, something serious is wrong. No, in my father and mother's house there was much general gay conversation all over the place.

Q: I was harkening back to when I first knew the Harts and they had dinner parties, this was the case.* With the change in

---

*Captain Thomas C. Hart, USN, served as chief ordnance inspector in charge of the torpedo station from 1927 to 1929.

course, you changed conversation with your other partner. But that's passed out now, too.

Mrs. Smith: Well, heavens, yes. Gosh! Besides, you can't imagine being so rude, sit and talk to one fellow all the time. Well, the Harts were in command at the station when we got there.

Q: This was up in Newport.

Mrs. Smith: Newport.

Q: And the date of that was when?

Mrs. Smith: 1928.

Q: This was you and your husband?

Mrs. Smith: Yes, he was there on duty. We'd just come back from China and brought the powder monkey. Do you know what a powder monkey is?

Q: No, I don't know what a powder monkey is.

Mrs. Smith: Well, I've just been reading Roy's book here,

Yangtze Patrol, which is fascinating to me.*

Q: Kemp Tolley's book.

Mrs. Smith: Yes, fascinating. He's full of humor, and it's all the roots of when we were out there, what was going on. Of course, my husband was at Nanking. It gives a long account of that. But Roy was on the ship because we had Admiral Williams as our admiral and he wouldn't allow us to travel on a transport.**

Q: Was this Henry Williams?

Mrs. Smith: Clarence, I think his name was. But his wife went up on the Isabel with friends, but the rest of us poor things went up at our own expense. So we thought this would be fine. We put Roy, who was then 14, on the ship, the Noa, and went up to Shanghai, and I was to follow up and pick him off, you see. The ship got to Shanghai, and was immediately sent upriver. They had the big Nanking blow-up, and Roy was on board all the time. Powder monkey in the old British Navy, and I suppose other navies, they had boys in their early teens, 12, 13, 14, aboard ship, and they helped serve the guns. Whatever they brought, I

---
*Rear Admiral Kemp Tolley, USN, Yangtze Patrol: The U.S. Navy in China (Annapolis: Naval Institute Press, 1971). Admiral Tolley's oral history is included in the Naval Institute's collection.
**Admiral Clarence S. Williams, USN, Commander in Chief, U.S. Asiatic Fleet from 1925 to 1927.

wouldn't know. In those days, guns were muzzle-loaded. Yes, because that's one of the things that my father and his friends did, changed over from muzzle-loading to breech-loading, the new big-gun stuff. But Roy was there, 14, busy in the middle of it all. You can imagine. And according to Mr. Tolley, he's the last living powder monkey. There aren't any more, you know. Nobody does that anymore. And he had a ball.

Well, I don't know, the Naval Academy in those days, of course, it just seemed perfectly normal. There was the corrals, as they call them, which are two blocks of flats, apartments, which were right where the officers' club is, a little closer to the pavement, and the Cluveriuses were there.* He was my husband's uncle. He married Miss Sampson, you see. And the hospital was beyond it. And then I don't remember anything much beyond that.

Q: The hospital was not where it is now?

Mrs. Smith: Gosh, no. It was right there.

Q: That was water in those days, I suppose.

Mrs. Smith: It was being finished off as what they called Oklahoma, all that land which is a beautiful place, you know, and in between, the hospital was more or less where the club is.

---
*Admiral Wat T. Cluverius, Jr., USN.

See, first there were two big apartment houses, fairly big. I think they had four apartments. And then beyond that, there was a walk, and then there was a hospital down there. I don't remember it particularly. I hadn't any great thing to do with it, you might say.

Q: What about living in these compound arrangements, what about the entertaining between families, that sort of thing? Did you do much of that?

Mrs. Smith: Of course, I didn't.

Q: No, but your family.

Mrs. Smith: My family did. I don't remember that they did a great deal. No, it wasn't any buzz-buzz-buzz business at all, no. When they had a party, it was a formal dinner, a very formal dinner. People dressed. Well, even when we got back, I was thinking about it the other day, when we got back to Newport . . .

Q: It was still formal?

Mrs. Smith: Well, I mean, you thought nothing of asking people—they used to have so many dances a year. The Torpedo Station had a dance and Fort Adams had a dance, the War College had a dance.

You asked people to dinner, and you thought nothing of their wearing white tie and tails. Can you imagine asking anybody to dinner, just casual in your house? You know.

Q: What kind of entertainment, then, when you were not going to a dance, at a dinner party at home?

Mrs. Smith: You mean in the early days of the Naval Academy?

Q: Yes. In the home, when you invited people to dinner, did you have any special kind of entertainment?

Mrs. Smith: Well, when we lived in Blake Row, you have to remember, I was not in the entertainment era.

Q: No, you were shunted off to bed?

Mrs. Smith: Upstairs with a book, you know. My family were great readers. But certainly I wasn't welcome at any dinner party at 12 and 13, you know. I had nothing to do with it.

Q: I wonder was there any music or anything like that at a dinner party when you had a fancy one in the home.

Mrs. Smith: No, no.

Q: Just conversation.

Mrs. Smith: Just lots of conversation. No, no. And when we lived in Sampson Row, which was later, my father and mother were very fond of music, and they used to go every year to the opera in New York. Father had one of the very first phonographs, and they used to have music parties, because he had records of Caruso and de Reszke and all those people, you know, and they used to ask people to dinner and listen to records.* There wasn't any TV. There wasn't any radio. They used to do that, people that were fond of music. Mostly the people just talked.

Q: There were musical events in Annapolis itself, too, were there not, up at the State House, the Governor's Mansion, and that sort of thing?

Mrs. Smith: The first governor I remember was Ritchie, and I don't remember anything about him except he was considered very wild and rapid.**

Q: Because he didn't have a wife.

Mrs. Smith: No, he didn't have a wife. He had a mother, and I

---

*Enrico Caruso, Italian tenor with the Metropolitan Opera Company; Jean de Reszke, Polish tenor.
**Albert C. Ritchie, governor of Maryland from 1920 to 1924.

have a friend now, who is 90, who used to go to his parties. They used to have lots to drink and used to run around and be really gay, you know.

Q: I'm thinking, Caroline Hart was telling me that in the town there were various families who had what they called musicals, and they would invite people in for it.*

Mrs. Smith: Well, they did. Undoubtedly my father and mother went, and undoubtedly I couldn't have cared less or paid any attention. I had four brothers and sisters in the house, and the house was full of people, as you might say, and you did your own thing. You didn't go out in the evening, gosh knows.

Q: You did a lot of reading, you say?

Mrs. Smith: Yes, I did. I used to love the old library. Where was it? It was down there near Stribling Road, now where--I forget what the building is. At the foot of Maryland Avenue, it used to be the engineering building, where they made the heat for the whole yard. Beyond that was a giant coal pile, and the library was ahead of that, up towards the chapel from that. And then the library, of course, was put in. I don't know if it's still there, in--what did we call that? What's the building? It

---

*Caroline Brownson Hart, daughter of Captain Willard H. Brownson, USN, Superintendent of the Naval Academy from 1902 to 1905.

isn't Sampson Hall.

Q: Mahan Hall?

Mrs. Smith: No, the building that's down below the library, below the museum.

Q: Sampson is one, and then Mahan.

Mrs. Smith: Well, the center used to be the library.

Q: Yes, I know that, until the Nimitz Library was built. It was the library.

Mrs. Smith: Yes. Well, that was new then, because I used to read a lot, yes, I did. My father had the theory that no matter what you read, the more you read, the better, because your taste would inevitably improve, so that my brothers were allowed to read those Nick Carter things, which are now priceless. You can sell them for heaps of money. Then they cost five cents, and all his friends used to pour into the house, because they weren't allowed to read them. You know. I can see pictures of them now. I thought they were dull. You know the virtuous one always had long, lovely blonde hair, and the bad one always had black hair.

Q: Yes, naturally.

Mrs. Smith: Yes, naturally. I don't know why blondes are considered so virtuous. I don't know, I'm sure the Academy didn't buzz with gaiety, and the Harts were--well, when we knew them at the Torpedo Station, were still quite stiff and formal. They had--I remember their living room was as bare as if they just moved in. I mean, there was no knickknacks and personal doings around. It was just government. That's the way I remember it, at least. I may have misjudged it, because we used to go there occasionally. I remember we were busy getting people on the island, getting busy to have our party, you know, in turn, a Torpedo Station party to match the War College and the rest of them. And Admiral Hart was talking to us, to the wives there, and saying, "Of course, everything we do will undoubtedly turn out to be wrong." I thought that was the most awful point of view to begin with.

Q: What was his . . .

Mrs. Smith: I said to him afterwards, I said, "Listen, you talk like that, you aren't going to get any real volunteers' enthusiasm, because you've squashed them before you begin."

Q: What did he say to that?

Mrs. Smith: He disapproved. He disapproved of me from the day I laughed at him when he was stuck in the mud. I think he always did, and I said to Roy, "I'm not sure he ever forgave me. Because when you were naughty at the Academy, Admiral Hart said that naval children, naval sons, should understand discipline like nobody else." He eased out all the naval boys that he could. I mean, a whole bunch of them have done extremely well since. It seems sort of too bad because the things they did were not so evil and awful. One of the terrible things Roy did was he swam in the pool. He was on the water polo team, and they sneaked down one hot night—one night, anyway—and went swimming in the pool. Just dreadful. And the watchman said to me, "Of course, I recognized him." So he built up a great wall of demerits. We were in Panama. We couldn't do much about it. Screaming at him didn't help.* In those days, I don't think people did all this buzz-buzz. They stayed home.

Q: Of course, they didn't have the opportunity.

Mrs. Smith: I mean, for instance, at the Academy, I don't know if there was all this madly running to and fro. There may have been, but I don't think so.

Q: Did you ride horseback?

---

*Mrs. Smith's son, Midshipman Roy C. Smith III, USN, Naval Academy class of 1934, was dismissed from the Academy in December 1933. He went on to graduate from the University of Michigan and retired from the Navy as a captain in the reserves.

Mrs. Smith: Me? Heavens, no. Who ever heard of a horse?

Q: The Brownsons had horses there.

Mrs. Smith: Did they?

Q: Oh, yes.

Mrs. Smith: I don't remember them.

Q: They had a stable of horses.

Mrs. Smith: Did they? Where? Must have been out of town.

Q: I think out in town. Because they all rode.

Mrs. Smith: Well, they must have had it out in town, and that was way over my head, as you might say. Mrs. Marble, George Marble's wife, had a horse in town, because when we lived in 5 Maryland Avenue, she had a--I don't know what you would call it, you can hardly call it a stable--she kept a horse right back of us. She rode. They used to ride to hounds, if you please. I don't know where.

Q: Talk about your courtship.

Mrs. Smith: My family disapproved heartily. They said, "You're much too young.

Q: Where were you when you met your husband-to-be?

Mrs. Smith: I had come home from boarding school, and I was living in 5 Maryland Avenue with the family. And I met millions of midshipmen, as you can imagine, you know, lots of them. And I met him, as I remember, in Catherine Devalier's house. She had a party, tea party, like we used to have, and you met midshipmen that way. Then, of course, my father had a lot of classmates who had sons who came or came with recommendations to him, and you know, but I didn't think they were very interesting that way. I mean, you don't want to have them brought to you on a plate, so to speak. But I remember Catherine lived in the old--what was it? The old--I can't think of the name--house on Prince George Street, and we had a wonderful time. Once we went out there and camped overnight in a tent.

Q: In the back yard?

Mrs. Smith: In the back yard. Catherine and I and, I guess, I forget who, I guess probably Karen Steele, Karen Welsh now.

Q: You sound like Boy Scouts.

Mrs. Smith: Well, we were very enterprising, and Hall--Margaret was too starchy to bother with us, but Juli came and tormented us, hung over the fence and yelled at us, you know, Margaret's brother, Julius. But I think people were--I don't know what they did in the evening. I think they probably--in my family, everybody had a book.

Q: And read, yes.

Mrs. Smith: Everybody had a book.

Q: And that was good, too, wasn't it? You started telling me about meeting your husband-to-be.

Mrs. Smith: Oh, nothing. I met him.

Q: At a tea party.

Mrs. Smith: Yes, tea party. No matter who you were, Superintendent or anybody else, there was nothing to drink but tea. Not even coffee. Tea. I met him and then I was--what was I? I guess I was 17, 18, and I met a lot of other rivals, as you might say. And then we decided we'd like to be engaged and the family had a fit. My mother said . . .

Q: What class was he?

Mrs. Smith: 1910. So that gives you a funny feeling, too. Now here's Pete Mitscher, the great Mitscher, you know, the aviator with the ship named for him and all that stuff.* He was as bad as Roy. In those days, you lost your September leave if you got too many demerits. The iron-fisted Hart wasn't there. You lost your September leave, and you had to be there all of September. He had the reputation of being what they called a "red mike," who didn't go out with girls. I don't know why he went out with me, but he used to ask me to go sailing every afternoon. He was great fun, he really was.

Q: That was Harry Hill's class, too, wasn't it?**

Mrs. Smith: Harry was '11, and he was a great basketball player, big thrill, you know. I used to know him. I used to know some of the people in 1909 because long around then, my father gave me a boat, a little light sort of skiff thing, you know. We used to go out in that and go crabbing and row around to the end of the harbor there where those monitors, you know, a freeboard about that high; there were two of them out there. And in the afternoon, they had the Alvarado and the Sandoval, which were captured Spanish gunboats, I guess, and they used to go out in

---

*Midshipman Marc A. Mitscher, USN, Naval Academy class of 1910, who distinguished himself during World War II as a fast carrier task force commander. The reminiscences of his wife, Frances, are contained in this volume.
**Midshipman Harry W. Hill, USN, who as a vice admiral served as Superintendent from 1950 to 1952.

turn in the afternoon on summer days, take a turn.* Anybody in the Academy could go. I didn't know many people outside, except my special friend. You could go aboard and take a cruise down the bay in the afternoon, you and the children or the nurse and the children or whatever you like. It was very pleasant.

Q: Was the Mercedes there then?**

Mrs. Smith: No, the Santee was there. Then the Santee departed and the Reina appeared.*** What was that lovely sailing ship, was there, too. What was she, the Chesapeake?**** I don't remember. I remember my father taking me by the hand and saying, "I want to show you something interesting." And he said, "This

---

*USS Alvarado and USS Sandoval, steel gunboats captured in the summer of 1898 upon the Spanish surrender, served as training ships at the Naval Academy until 1906.

**USS Reina Mercedes (IX-25) was assigned to the Naval Academy from 1912 to 1957, first as housing for midshipmen undergoing punishment and then from 1940 on as a barracks ship for enlisted personnel assigned to the Academy. Because the commander of the nearby North Severn naval station, who also was captain of the ship, was provided quarters for his family aboard, this was the only U.S. naval ship in which dependents were allowed to live.

***USS Santee, a 44-gun frigate that served the U.S. Navy in the Civil War, was assigned to the Naval Academy during the latter part of its wartime stay in Newport. Upon the Academy's return to Annapolis, the Santee was used as a gunnery training ship and barracks for punished midshipmen until April 1912 when she sank at her mooring and was later scrapped.

****The steel-hulled square-rigger Chesapeake was used for midshipmen summer cruises from 1900 until 1907 (having been renamed Severn in 1904). She was retained at the Academy as a drill ship until 1910.

is the first submarine, the <u>Holland</u>," which was that big.* An intelligent whale, they called it, you know. I think Roy had it at his museum in Washington.**

Q: An intelligent whale.

Mrs. Smith: Well, it looked like that, you know. And Pa said, "Some day these are going to be very important to the world," you know, but you wouldn't have thought so to look at it. It looked like nothing.

I don't know, from there we just went on, you know, went to dancing and things like that. And, of course, in those days, midshipmen couldn't be married until they'd been out for two years. You graduated as a passed midshipmen, then you became an ensign, with an enormous pay of something like $200 a month, if that. I don't remember. And so we were married. I was 20 and he was 24, I guess.

Q: But you became engaged while he was still a midshipman?

Mrs. Smith: Well, yes. I guess his first class year. As I say,

---

*The 54-foot USS <u>Holland</u> (SS-1) was based at the Naval Academy from 1900 until 1905.
**Between 1966 and 1970, Captain Roy C. Smith III, USNR(Ret.) was director of the Navy-Marine Corps Memorial Museum in Washington, D.C. The <u>Holland</u> (SS-1) was struck from the Navy records in 1910 and sold for scrap in 1913. The Intelligent Whale, unsuccessful predecessor of the <u>Holland</u>, is on display at the Navy-Marine Corps Memorial Museum.

the family had a fit. They said, "You're too young, you're too young." And his family had a fit, "You're too young, you're too young.

We said, "To hell with you all."

Q: But they approved of him otherwise, did they?

Mrs. Smith: Well, they could hardly not, because after all, in those days, the Navy proudly called themselves a band of brothers. They really were, and they all knew each other. The Navy was small, and my father and Captain Smith knew each other, and they knew the Sampsons. I know when I was growing up, my uncle, Montgomery Taylor, was with Dewey in the Battle of Manila Bay, and the air was full of grandma worrying, you know, and my other uncle, who was in 14th Infantry at the Boxer business.* And it seemed to me there was always a ship in the background and somebody worrying about it. But that didn't worry me. Did it worry you? Did you have any brothers and sisters?

Q: Yes.

Mrs. Smith: Did it worry you, what went on with them? After

---

*Lieutenant Montgomery M. Taylor, USN. As a full admiral in the early 1930s, Taylor served as Commander in Chief, Asiatic Fleet; Commodore George Dewey, USN, commanded the Asiatic Squadron that destroyed the Spanish fleet off Cavite on 1 May 1898 with no U.S. losses; the 1900 Boxer Rebellion occurred when a secret, revolutionary organization of Chinamen seized Peking and attempted to oust all foreign legations. U.S. troops joined an international expedition which restored order to the city.

you've grown up, you took an interest, but when they were young, you just thought, "Who are they?" You know. If anybody asked you exactly what they did, could you tell them? You might, I don't know.

Q: Well, anyway, your romance developed, but you had to wait.

Mrs. Smith: We had to wait two years. Everybody had to wait two years.

Q: Until he became an ensign. Then where were you married? At the chapel at the Academy?

Mrs. Smith: No, no, no. We were married in the house. My father died in February.

Q: He had been stationed in Washington?

Mrs. Smith: Well, he was stationed in Washington and here. At least he was secretary-treasurer of the Naval Institute. And he was also on a board in Washington, ordnance board. He could live either place, you see.

Q: But the commuting was difficult, wasn't it?

Mrs. Smith: Well, the train went up, and then they put in the

WB&A, which ran around town, enormous clacking thing, you know.*

Q: Yes, the old electric.

Mrs. Smith: And you could take that and you could go to Washington, but in the beginning, you took the train at West Street and went to Odenton, changed, because I went up with him a couple of times. At Odenton, you changed into another train, but I don't know whether he minded or not. He never made any comments about it. And everybody walked everywhere.

Q: It was the only way to do it.

Mrs. Smith: Yes. I mean, we certainly didn't have any carriage, and he certainly didn't ride a bicycle out to the station, so he must have walked. Everybody did. Nobody thought a thing of walking. And you sent notes, you know, to people. You didn't telephone. At least in the beginning you didn't. It was all so different, and it seemed perfectly natural.

Q: Did you pay postage on notes?

Mrs. Smith: No, you'd send a maid or somebody with a note.

Q: Hand-delivered notes.

---

*WB&A--Washington, Baltimore, and Annapolis Railroad.

Mrs. Smith: Yes, we had an old colored man whose name was Byas, who used to--well, in those days, everybody had servants, you know. Ma had a cook and a waitress, and my two sisters were both young; they each had a nurse because they were very different. I don't know why they both had nurses, but they did. I thought they were a big nuisance, all of them. Of course, we had Byas, who polished the knives, which you did in those days because they were steel and they had to be polished, and they blacked the shoes. The only heat in the house were those LaTroupe stoves, you know. Those had to be serviced.

Q: Coal-burning.

Mrs. Smith: Yes, coal. Sure.

Q: Did you have fireplaces, too?

Mrs. Smith: Well, Pa put in a furnace when we moved there, so we had steam heat.

Q: Oh, you were privileged to have central heat.

Mrs. Smith: We did, we had central heat. And we had a telephone, too. We were very advanced, I'm telling you.

Q: Was it a wall type thing? The telephone, was it on the wall?

Mrs. Smith: Oh, no, of course not. It wasn't on the wall. Certainly not. It stood up on a thing like that, like you see in antique stores, a stem like this. I don't remember ever using it. Who would I call, as you might say? My friends didn't have them. You walked. If I was going to Murray Hill, for instance--Caroline lived in Murray Hill--you walked. If she went to a hop, she walked home. Natch. And she had an uncle, Sam Brooks, who used to be in the bank, who's a bachelor, who used to come down and meet the Murray Hill girls and walk home with them because the midshipmen couldn't.

Q: But there was no danger of being mugged or anything in those days.

Mrs. Smith: Well, it wasn't for a long time. Oh, ages after that I used to come and stay with my mother and go out. I used to play mah-jongg a lot, and we used to go out and play. Oh, Nancy Gearing and Mrs. Almy, I forget who, but various people, and we used to walk home at night, not think anything about it. Later we took the car, you know.

Q: You said your father was secretary-treasurer.

Mrs. Smith: Secretary-treasurer of the Naval Institute.

Q: Tell me about that.

Mrs. Smith: What they call the <u>Proceedings</u>. All I know about that is that it was a small official--you know what I mean, not official, but technical--what's the word?

Q: Professional magazine.

Mrs. Smith: Professional magazine. And he took it over.

Q: Where was it located? Where were the offices?

Mrs. Smith: The offices were right about where the museum is, as I remember. I'm not sure where the offices were. I'm not sure, but it was still going when I was married. I was married in 1912, you see. It was still going, because Mr. Conroy then was the head man, and my father, of course, had died in February.* And he came out and told my mother that anything he could do he'd be glad to, so Ma gave him all the wedding invitations. We had announcements because I was married in the house. My mother preferred it that way, and I couldn't have cared less. So we were married in the bay window there at 5 Maryland Avenue. And my uncle, Montgomery Taylor, gave me away. Being a bachelor, he had worse fits than I, and I wasn't having any fits at all.

Q: How much time did your father spend at the Naval Institute?

---

*James W. Conroy, the Naval Institute's first permanent staff member, served for 40 years beginning in 1883, running it single-handedly for six months during the Spanish-American War.

Mrs. Smith: His week was divided. He came and went. I think he went to Washington twice a week, perhaps, but I don't really remember. When you were growing up . . .

Q: That was not a part of your life, actually.

Mrs. Smith: No. When you were growing up, did you remember when your father went to the office or didn't go to the office or where he went and what he did? We didn't pay any attention. That was his--you know, when he was home, he was always very gay, lots of fun, and when he was home, the whole atmosphere of the house was gay and merry. My grandmother came and lived with us after a while, and she was very serious-minded, so that the devil was down, Pa's home was up. I ran around in between them, minding my own business. My life was very full with me. I'd worry about what dress to be in. It didn't bother me at all. We lived right opposite old Mrs. Phythian, the widow of whatever he was, Commodore, Admiral Phythian, long since dead.* She was an old lady, and Mrs. Bookwalter, whose husband was a naval officer, and Mrs. Pringle, Admiral Pringle's wife.** I don't know why they were there, but they were there. In the afternoon, it was then the fashion you went out and sat on your front steps, at least they did, and every summer afternoon, they'd open up the

---
*Commodore Robert L. Phythian, USN (Ret.), who died on 22 January 1917. As a captain, Phythian was Superintendent of the Naval Academy from 1890 to 1894.
**Mrs. Charles S. Bookwalter; Mrs. Joel R. Pringle.

front door, and Mrs. Pringle would sit at the head of the steps in her rocking chair, Bonnie Thompson on one side. Bonnie Thompson's name is Buenavista for Zachary Taylor's thing, and he was my grandfather's uncle.* But Mrs. Bookwalter sat on one side, and Mrs. Pringle sat on the other steps, and Bonnie sat there, too, and nothing passed them. Cordelia Pringle is Cordelia Kane. There were two granddaughters both named Cordelia, Cordelia Bookwalter and Cordelia Pringle. And she's now Cordelia Kane, and she is the mother of Jack Kane in Washington.**

Q: Oh, really?

Mrs. Smith: Her husband was coming back from the Orient during the war and he fell, or jumped, nobody ever knew, down the hatch and was killed.*** He was coming back with battle fatigue or whatever you want to call it, and I don't know how you fall down the hatch, but he did, anyway, and was killed. And their son Jack was a friend of my younger son's, who died, and he is now in

---

*Zachary Taylor (1784-1850) was the 12th President of the United States (1849-1850) and hero of the Mexican War. In February 1847, Major General Taylor, USA, led his troops in the defeat of Santa Anna at Buena Vista, Mexico, though they were outnumbered 4 to 1, ending the northern campaign of the Mexicans.
**Rear Admiral John D. Kane, Jr., USN (Ret.), who was recalled to active duty in December 1976 to serve as Director of Naval History, a position he held until his second retirement in November 1985.
***Captain John D. Kane, USN, died 13 June 1944 from a fall suffered aboard the ship he commanded, USS New Orleans (CA-32).

Washington.* I tell you, it gives you a very odd feeling to have your son's children retired admirals, because I grew up in a nest of admirals. I mean, cousin Jack and cousin Lizzy, Admiral John and his wife who lived at the side of the hill, and there was Cousin Fred, who I discovered all four of them, John Rodgers, Willie Rodgers, Fred Rodgers, and, of course, my uncle Montgomery Taylor, were all chief--what do you call it?**

Q: Chief engineers?

Mrs. Smith: No, the South--listen to me. The Pacific Fleet.

Q: Commander in Chief.

Mrs. Smith: Commander in Chief Pacific Fleet. No, not Pacific Fleet, that's on this coast. The Asiatic Fleet.

Q: The Asiatic Fleet, way out.

Mrs. Smith: Yes, but as I said, there was Cousin Jack, Cousin

---

*Mrs. Smith's youngest child, Montgomery, died on 16 September 1975.

**The distinguished Rodgers family of American flag officers descended from Colonel John Rodgers and his wife Elizabeth Reynolds Rodgers. Rear Admiral John Rodgers, USN, commanded the Asiatic Squadron from 1870 to 1872; Rear Admiral Frederick Rodgers, USN, held the position in 1902. Under the new title of Commander in Chief, Asiatic Fleet, Rear Admiral William L. Rodgers, USN, filled the billet from 1918 to 1919, and Admiral Montgomery M. Taylor, USN, from 1930 to 1933.

Fritz, Cousin Willie--they all turned into admirals eventually. And, of course, my Uncle Mont was not an admiral then, none of them were. I don't know what their rank was. As far as I was concerned, they were antiques.

Q: Was that the Christopher Raymond Perry Rodgers family?

Mrs. Smith: Yes. The one I just christened the ship for. I just came back from Mississippi last Saturday.

Q: Pascagoula.

Mrs. Smith: Pascagoula, and christened the new John Rodgers, and she's named for the commodore, his son, and his grandson, great-grandson, whatever it is, who was number two aviator.* I knew him more or less; he was older than me and of no interest to me at all. But he was in and out, you know. In fact, they were here on duty. I don't know what he was doing, but they were here for a bit because his wife used to come in and talk to Ma. And then, of course, when I got married, I acquired Admiral Sampson, Admiral Cluverius, and Admiral Jackson. So there have always been . . .

---

*The USS John Rodgers (DD-983) was named for Commodore John Rodgers, USN (1772-1838), his son Rear Admiral John Rodgers, USN (1812-1882), the latter's nephew Rear Admiral John A. Rodgers, USN (1848-1933), and his son Commander John Rodgers, (1881-1926), Naval Aviator #2. The John Rodgers was christened by Mrs. Smith on 18 March 1978, and commissioned on 14 July 1979.

Q: The Admiral Jackson, Richard Jackson?*

Mrs. Smith: He was my husband's uncle. He married Miss Sampson. Admiral Sampson had a daughter married Jackson, daughter married Smith, daughter married Cluverius, another daughter married Scott in the Army. **

Q: Did you have any Howards in your family background, too?

Mrs. Smith: None that I ever heard of. No, no, we had lots of Taylors because my grandfather--wait a minute. Zachary Taylor was my grandfather's uncle.

Q: The President.

Mrs. Smith: Yes, the President. So we had lots of Taylors. Virginia Taylors are all related. Heaps of them. Because Roy is a Cincinnati on that account, and my daughter Mary is what they call "daughters of Cin." She's a lady Cincinnati on another line, you see. I mean, to be a Cincinnati, you have to be a descendent, I think it is . . .

Q: Of the Revolutionary War, isn't it?***

---

*Admiral Richard H. Jackson, USN.
**Admiral Wat T. Cluverius, Jr., USN.
***The Society of Cincinnati is the exclusive veterans organization from the American Revolution formed by American and French officers in 1873. Each veteran inducted into the society is followed by one descendent at a time.

Mrs. Smith: Yes, Revolutionary War. But the family began in the Revolutionary War, and the beginning of the Navy, the beginning of West Point. They were in there, both, so they've been fighters ever since when.

Q: Do you have any Mustins in your family tree?

Mrs. Smith: No. No. The Navy ones were Rodgers. Christopher Raymond Perry was--I don't know how he came in, because originally there was an old Scotsman who came and set up an inn at Havre de Grace, and his son was the first commodore Rodgers, who fought the Barbary pirates and saved Baltimore from the British.

Q: That was the War of 1812.

Mrs. Smith: Yes. And Baltimore gave them an enormous silver service, which is in a museum somewhere, I guess. And his son did--I've got the thing written down from Pascagoula if you want to see it.

Q: Let's get back to your early married life now. You were married in 1912 in Annapolis.

Mrs. Smith: It was a dud, in a sense, because, you see, off he went to sea, and Roy was born in 1913.

Q: Where did you live?

Mrs. Smith: Well, I had to live with Ma.

Q: In Annapolis.

Mrs. Smith: Listen, I think I had $100 a month and Pa had $75, or something like that. We had nothing, you know. No. It was the custom then . . .

Q: A hundred dollars went a long way.

Mrs. Smith: Yeah, but not that long. In those days, it was the custom, when Pa was at sea, if you were lucky enough to have a home, you lived at home, which is what I did, you see, and Roy was born. Then, of course, the ships went up to Newport, and I went up there and dragged Roy along, and eventually took Mary along in the summer. Then, of course . . .

Q: That was very difficult, wasn't it, to move around?

Mrs. Smith: And don't think the government paid your way, because it didn't.

Q: It did not pay your way?

Mrs. Smith: It didn't pay one damn cent.

Q: How did you get up there, by train?

Mrs. Smith: You went by your little self by train. And me, having before that been sent--when I went up, we had friends up there and I stayed at the Portsmouth Yard with a friend of mine whose father was captain of the yard, and I went up in a drawing room under the special care of the porter, you know what I mean, was met and so on. The next thing that happens to me is I'm going up with Roy, who weighed 1,000 pounds, and I couldn't put him in the upper berth; he might fall out. So I had to sleep with him overnight, and that's wild, I'm telling you. We finally get to Newport. In those days, you landed on the other side and took the ferry. We went over and stayed in Jamestown, that kind of thing. Gee, it was a long time ago.

Q: Pretty hectic and pretty demanding on a Navy wife, wasn't it?

Mrs. Smith: Yes, it was tough, I tell you. The only thing that got us being transported even to the home port was the war. When all the people who came in from civil life screamed bloody murder, and of course, the Army could go places. If you were sent to a post, you had a house. But we were orphans of the storm, out in the breezes, and very few naval people could afford to go--wives, I mean. You stayed home. And if the government did send you, it sent you to the home port. Now they might send me to the home port in Boston. The ship might spend its time in California. That doesn't affect the Navy Department at all. Then, of course, the war came.

Q: World War I.

Mrs. Smith: And what I had to do was, I came up to Jamestown in the summer, having saved up madly all winter, you might say. I spent most of my time at my mother's. My father had died and she moved out to Southgate Avenue and had a house, and I lived there until he came home. He came home and sometimes I'd get away and go see him for a weekend but not very often, because I couldn't leave the kids, you know. Then finally there is the war, and he's in the South Carolina, and they're on duty, the ship is down at Hampton Roads or Portsmouth, wherever it was.* And all of a sudden, he's ordered off that onto the SS Luckenbach, which is an ordinary, everyday merchant ship.

Mrs. Smith: And he and one sailor and one--by this time, I guess, he was a lieutenant. He was only a lieutenant commander when he had command of a ship in China. I guess he was a lieutenant then, though, and he and a sailor and one slightly senior gent and what you might call a pop gun were sent out on

---

*The individual in the South Carolina was Mrs. Smith's husband, Lieutenant Roy C. Smith, Jr., USN.

the <u>Luckenbach</u> as armed guard, Admiral Gleaves's first armed guard.* And there were nests of submarines out, because, you know, security didn't exist. Fortunately they didn't meet one. They got safely over to Saint Nazaire, and they unloaded all the ammunition they had taken.

Q: It was an ammunition ship?

Mrs. Smith: It was carrying ammunition, yes.

Q: Unescorted?

Mrs. Smith: It was the escort.

Q: It was the escort?

Mrs. Smith: Sure. It was escorting others. It had one--I don't know how big the gun was.

Q: One gun.

Mrs. Smith: I'm sure the gun was very small, and submarines were bigger than the Intelligent Whale but not terribly big--not like today, certainly. They got to Saint Nazaire and unloaded the

---

*Rear Admiral Albert Gleaves, USN, Commander Atlantic Fleet Cruiser and Transport Force from July 1917 to December 1918.

ammunition and discovered--I don't know how much they unloaded, but they discovered that it didn't fit any of the guns they had over there, so they reloaded it and brought it back. And my husband, having lived abroad, his father was a naval attache in Paris for a while, and even an attache in Russia at the court, and why he didn't keep any interesting notes, I don't know, but he didn't. So anyway, my husband went to school abroad and spoke French fluently, and he thought it would be lovely to be able to stay over there and be an interpreter and be in the middle of things, you know. But he wasn't. He came back.

Q: He had to be guard on the boat.

Mrs. Smith: Well, he had to run the thing. He came back, and then they made another trip and still, thank God, didn't meet any submarines. They had some little excitement but didn't actually meet anything. And this time he was in command. They went over and again they came back safely, and this is very agitating.

Q: This time they had the right ammunition, did they?

Mrs. Smith: I guess. I don't know what they took that time, but it was very agitating for wives because the newspapers would say, "Extra! Extra! Extra! Ship Sunk! Ship Sunk!" And they never gave out the name of the ship because, you see . . .

Q: To buy the paper.

Mrs. Smith: Oh, no, the paper didn't tell you, certainly not. It was dead secret, because they didn't want the enemy to know. So you had no more idea than the dead whether your ship had gone down or not. You had to wait until the Navy Department would let you know if he was dead. It was gay, I tell you. If you heard an, "Extra! Extra!" you nearly died.

So the next time he went, two trips, came back that time, and to his wrath and fury, decoded his own orders to the Naval Academy to teach midshipmen. He nearly died.

Q: It was something he did not want to do?

Mrs. Smith: Well, he wanted to stay in the war. So anyway, he rushed up to Washington, along with various others, and said, "Listen, I don't want to do that. I want to stay at sea. I want to stay at sea."

They said, "Shut up and go back and teach midshipmen. It's very important." It nearly killed him.

I said to him, "I never thought the first time we had a house or lived anywhere, that you'd be in a rage all the time about it."

Q: He was wanting to get away.

Mrs. Smith: "I was hoping when you finally got ashore it would be lovely," you know. Well, he naturally had to settle down and accept his fate.

Q: Where did you have your house?

Mrs. Smith: We lived on King George Street in those funny little houses. I don't know if they've changed now, little wooden houses almost opposite Ogle Hall, a little further down.* The corner house was an old brick house faced on Maryland Avenue, and then there were three little ones. And Mrs. Oldendorf lived in the house next to us, and her sister Mrs. Brown.** Then there was an old boatswain retired and his wife and child. She, Rosie, was a great pal of Roy's. The Oldendorf girl was a little older, rather starchy, and Rosie and Roy played around together, and then they went to Baltimore, scared the life out of us. They disappeared. They went out to play, you know. They were playing in the backyard and all that stuff, and I went to call them for lunch and there was no signs of them, none.

Q: Two little kids?

---

*Ogle Hall, a block from the Naval Academy in downtown Annapolis, was completed in 1739 and has been the home of three Maryland governors and of the descendants of Admiral David Dixon Porter. In 1944 the Porter family sold the property to the Naval Academy Alumni Association, and it is now referred to as the "Alumni House."

**Mrs. Jesse B. Oldendorf, whose husband distinguished himself as a cruiser division commander at Surigao Strait during the Battle of Leyte Gulf in October 1944.

Mrs. Smith: Two little kids; they were quite small, yes. I don't remember how big they were, but it was the last year of the war.

Q: 1917 or 1918.

Mrs. Smith: It was '18, I guess it was. Anyway, they vanished.

Q: Seven years old.

Mrs. Smith: I was petrified, and I rushed down to the yard and said at the gate, "Have you seen them?" Because Roy was then going to school. There was a little school in the Academy down about where the museum is. I don't really remember the geography. It's changed so, you know. And I rushed down and said to the old watchman, I said, "Have you seen my boy?"

He said, "No, no, I haven't." I had visions of him going down, knowing him, and falling over the sea wall and doing anything, you know. I ran all around the place and couldn't find him.

Came home and Mrs. Oldendorf said, "Oh, a message came from Baltimore from the Travelers' Aid people." Yes, exactly.

Roy had come to me before he disappeared and said he wanted some money to go and buy candy, and I said, "No, I'm not going to give you money for candy. No, what's the matter with you? Not now, anyway, certainly not." So anyway, that was the beginning, so to speak.

So Mrs. Oldendorf says that word had come through and that my colored maid, not knowing what to do with the call, had called her. They were right next door like this. And Travelers' Aid said, "Has anybody ever heard of a little boy named Roy Smith?"

She said, "Yes, he lives here."

So then I was to call back, so I did call back, and they said that they had a little boy and a little girl. They were there walking around the station. And the Travelers' Aid people saw them and felt they didn't quite look like waifs, and went over and talked to them. And Roy said his father had been home on a short leave, not then, but in the past, you know, and he said he was going to visit—his aunt had been there from New York, he was going to go visit his aunt.

Q: You mean he was going right on to New York?

Mrs. Smith: Yes, going on to New York just like that. And he was taking Rosie to visit, too, and he told them he was perfectly capable of taking care of Rosie and himself, too—beat it, you know. However, they did, thank God . . .

Q: Was this the candy money?

Mrs. Smith: He never got any candy money. Apparently what happened was after being turned down by me, he took Rosie by the hand and they walked out to the bank. He knew he had a savings account, a small one. You know how you do with small children, I mean, extra money, Christmas money or something. He went out to the Farmers Bank and they told them he couldn't draw it out unless he had his mother's permission or his father's permission. So they started back, and they were walking along College Avenue where the station used to be, the WB&A station was there. And Rosie was in the habit of going to Baltimore to visit her grandfather. Roy had never been on a train in his life. So they stopped to go in and look at the trains, you know, and they saw people getting on, and they just quietly got on. Nobody paid any attention to them. The conductor said afterwards he thought they were with people, never thought such calm children would do such things. So they rode peacefully to Baltimore, and thank heavens they didn't get off at a way station. They might have been lost for good.

Q: And they didn't pay anything then.

Mrs. Smith: Of course not. They got to Baltimore, you see. How do you expect to get on? Money didn't ever enter his life in those days, except five cents. So they were picked up by the Travelers' Aid and sent back. Very agitating for grandma. Me, grandma! I wasn't a grandma then. Rosie got whacked within an inch of her life, and I thought I was too modern for that kind of thing, so I talked to Roy about it, and the newspapers came out with a big hullaballoo and said "Small boy elopes." Had this big to-do about it.

Q: Eloped!

Mrs. Smith: Eloped with Rosie, you see. He had no idea of eloping with Rosie; they were just friends, just going along together peaceably, you know, seeing the world. So I caught him one day; he was hanging over the fence, and people were going by, "Hi! Hi, bridegroom."
    I said, "This is enough." So I took him in and whacked him.

Q: You weren't going to be so modern after all?

Mrs. Smith: No, no. So then we lived there. Then what did Cam do?* He went to sea. Where did he go to sea?

Q: Was he at the Academy for two years?

Mrs. Smith: Yes, just about. Yes, he was, because my youngest son was born in 1919, in the middle of the flu epidemic. I had it and it didn't seem to matter to Monty and me. And then we had to live somewhere. We had to buy a house on Southgate Avenue.

---

    *"Cam" refers to Mrs. Smith's husband, whose middle name was Campbell.

Q: In the meantime you had acquired furniture and all that, didn't you?

Mrs. Smith: We had nothing. No. In those days, the government didn't pay your way anywhere, and if it did, it paid to the home port and it didn't pay for any furniture that I remember. My contemporaries didn't own any furniture.

Q: When you set up a house in Annapolis.

Mrs. Smith: It was a furnished house.

Q: Oh, it was a furnished house.

Mrs. Smith: Furnished house. Then we bought a house and had no furniture. In fact, everybody of our age took great pains not to own anything, because if you did, you had to pay for it when it went anywhere, you know. Even after we retired, we had then to buy furniture because who in the world--well, there were a few rich people that did, but most people didn't, and now I listen to the young with interest. They buy houses, they sell houses. Wherever you go, you buy a house. We didn't do that.

Q: They make money as a result.

Mrs. Smith: Yes. Nobody dreamed of owning a house in my day.

Heaven's sakes, no. So then we lived on Southgate Avenue, and then he was in the King. I got a letter from a friend of mine down there, who says--oh, Cam was on leave, and he went back to the ship, and then I didn't hear from him for a couple of days. Then I got a letter from a friend of mine down there, Mrs. Boynton, and she says, "I think you should know that your husband is in the hospital very ill." Meanwhile, I had a note from the doctor that said, "Your husband wishes me to tell you that he's all right. He's just had a bad cold, not to worry."

Q: In the hospital.

Mrs. Smith: It didn't say he was in the hospital, it just said that, you see, just very noncommital. Then I had a letter from Thelma, so then I decided I would rush down. Of course, I hadn't any more money than a fly. So my grandmother kindly lent me $100 and I rushed across the street to Sam Brooks, who was in the bank, and he kindly went down to the bank and cashed me $100, and I took the train that night to Charleston, where the ship was, you see. And fortunately for me, his roommate's father, his old Naval Academy roommate's father, Admiral Anderson, was there in command.* And I don't know how she heard about it--I guess Mrs.

---

*Roy Smith, Jr.'s Naval Academy roommate was Lorain Anderson, whose father was Rear Admiral Edwin A. Anderson, USN, Commandant of the Charleston Navy Yard from 1919 to 1922. This incident occurred while Lieutenant Commander Smith was in the USS King (DD-242), which he commanded from 1920 to 1922.

Boynton told her, because I stayed with her. And the hospital was one of those war things, you know, and it was practically big, long, empty.

Q: Barracks type.

Mrs. Smith: Barracks type, and he was very ill. He had pneumonia. And the kind that Kerry got, I mean, I went to see him, I got there in the afternoon and Theda and I took the—we had to take the streetcar out to the hospital. I don't know where it was. It seemed to me forever. And the streetcar ran into an automobile, and those kids fell out, you know. I thought I'd had enough by that time, but still—and there was much screaming and goings-on, everybody jumped out of the streetcar, went out. I said to them, "Listen. I got enough on my plate. I can't do anything about these people, these children. I can't do anything with them." So the next thing I knew, Theda and I found ourselves running up the road as far as we could, carrying my suitcase. And a car came along, a hospital car, and picked us up and took us to the hospital. I rushed in to see him, and there he was in bed, really very ill, and sitting over here on a table was his breakfast tray untouched. And this was 2:00, 3:00 o'clock in the afternoon. I mean, loving care he got. So he began getting better. As soon as possible, I took him home to Annapolis and he had been ordered to duty at the Naval Academy.

Q: Back to the Naval Academy again?

Mrs. Smith: Yes, that's right, back to the Naval Academy again. That's right. And Henry B. Wilson was the admiral.*

Q: He must have been a successful teacher. They got him back again.

Mrs. Smith: Well, he was. He taught engineering. Not that he was crazy about it, I mean, about teaching there, but still, he was ordered back there. And then this was very annoying, because he went--I know what he did. When we got off the train, he was wobbly, as you can imagine. He insisted on going to the Navy Department and finding out, he was due for shore, what duty he was going to have. And he was supposed to go to the Naval Academy and they had a note there that he was not acceptable by Henry B. No reason. Who knew? This burned him to a crisp, because he'd been perfectly acceptable before.

Q: Had he known Admiral Wilson?

Mrs. Smith: Henry B? No. So we staggered home. The first thing he did was boil down to the Naval Academy to find out what was going on. Well, when we were in China, there was an R.C.

---

*Rear Admiral Henry B. Wilson, Superintendent of the Naval Academy from July 1921 to February 1925.

Smith. I don't know if his name was Roy or not. And we were always getting demanding bills and letters and things. Apparently he was a naval officer and he had a terrible character. He didn't pass his exams for commander or lieutenant, whatever it was. He didn't pass his exams, and he owed money all over the place. He'd run out on his wife and done everything.

Q: So they got confused.

Mrs. Smith: Henry B., without paying the slightest attention, had simply confused them. And he said to my husband, "Didn't you fail your exams?"

He said, "Certainly not. I got a commendation on it."

"And didn't you owe a lot of money?"

"Certainly not." So Henry B.--what was his name, the exec? I guess you call it exec.

Q: Commandant of Midshipmen?

Mrs. Smith: What was he? No, he was the Superintendent's right-hand staff.

Q: Exec, yes.

Mrs. Smith: Who was supposedly a great friend and admirer of my father-in-law's. You thought he might have taken the trouble in seeing the name, but he didn't. Kurtz.* But anyway, so that got cleared up finally, you know. We found that excessively annoying, because the mark was in the Navy Department that he was persona non grata at the Academy. They got all that straightened out. He was still pretty wobbly, but then he went on duty there. We had three years' duty there, and then we were ordered to China.

Q: He was fortunate it came along at that time when he was recovering.

Mrs. Smith: You're telling me. Then we were ordered from there to China. First he was supposed to go to a ship in Boston, and I was panicked. How in the world--what am I going to do in Boston with four kids? Where will I live? So he went up to Washington to find out where he was really going to go, and called me up and said, "You had better sit down."

I said, "Why?"

He said, "Because I've got some news for you. We're going to China." And he'd seen my Uncle Mont and his uncle Dick, I guess, and Admiral Jackson never had any children. He and his wife went all over the place together, you see. And they said, "Of course, Mary isn't going."

And he said, "How do you feel?"

I said, "If you think I want to sit here for three years [it

---
*Captain Thomas R. Kurtz, USN.

was a three-year stint] and bring up four children by myself and be a widow, you can think some more."

He said, "That's what I thought you'd say." So all right.

Then we had quite a busy time. We finally sold the car. We had an awful time doing it, because this man in Baltimore saw the ad and he kept coming down and trying to make me exchange it for a grand piano. I said, "The last thing I want is a grand piano." So finally we drew a dead horse and went, and that was all very exciting.*

Q: You went by what, transport?

Mrs. Smith: Well, in those days, Congress was a little less bold than they are today, and I think there were seven officers from the Academy, I forget exactly how many, who were all going out to China, Owen and---oh, I forget who all the others were. Zimmerman was one. We were all going out to China, and we were all ordered out on the Chaumont. Don't forget, this is the days of the Volstead Act. So a whole big push of congressmen, 20 or so, I think, decided that they would like to go out to China, and they wanted it.

Q: They were going on a junket.

---

*"Dead horse" is Navy slang for a loan which amounts to an advance against upcoming salary.

Mrs. Smith: They went on the <u>Chaumont</u> and we went commercially, which saved our lives because our dead horse, you see, it took us three weeks to get out there. We'd have had to pay a dollar and a half a day apiece, and this way, as Captain Guy Baker used to say, "Well, at least we have the free run of our teeth," as he put it.*

So we go out to China that way, you see, very salubriously, as you might say. We went up past the Aleutian Islands and so on, stopped in Japan. I thought there was trouble in China. Here they were talking about it, you know, the communists were beginning and Borodin carrying on.** There was much ado. And so I thought, "Well, perhaps it would be better to get off in Japan." And we didn't know what duty we were going to have, he was going to have--I say "we" because don't tell me wives don't have it, too. Maybe not aboard ship, but you know.

Q: You share and share alike.

Mrs. Smith: You do. After all, you're yanked here, yanked there, do without. But anyway, I went ashore in Japan along with

---
*Captain Guy E. Baker, USN. The Smiths made out very well on this trip. Because congressmen had priority over military dependents (and because the congressmen wanted to save money; they would have had to pay for commercial transportation themselves), the Smiths were bumped from the Navy transport and booked on a Dollar Line merchant ship at no cost to them. According to Captain Roy C. Smith III, USNR(Ret.), they had wonderful accommodations and five meals a day.
**Michael Borodin, chief Russian political advisor to the Chinese Communist Party.

my friend, Mrs. Baker, and she could afford it, she had nobody with her but one daughter. The hotels would take everything you had. I couldn't possibly afford that. So then we went on down to Shanghai, and the ship went over to Wusung, the other side of the river. And the lieutenant came down to the dock and gave everybody their orders. We didn't know if we were going to be China or Manila, up the river, where, what. So my husband's orders said that he would report the next morning, early, to the USS Rizal. He would go up to Chefoo and take command of the Noa. Rizal would send a ship's boat for him at 6:00 or 7:00 o'clock the next morning. This left us rather in a quandary because I had at least hoped he could go ashore and find me a place to live--not find it but help. So, of course, he packed all his stuff. You had your customs declaration at sea, and he had a gun, which he brought, which he insisted on bringing, just a small thing.

Q: Pistol.

Mrs. Smith: God knows why he had it, but he did, anyway, so it was all packed. And we went that night--I don't know how we managed, but we did try and get in touch with the Admiral McVay.*
He wanted to know if he could have a delay of 24 hours to see us ashore. The admiral said no. So, all right, the next morning at

---
*Rear Admiral Charles B. McVay, Jr., USN, Commander Yangtze Patrol.

the crack of dawn, he departs, bag and baggage.*

Q: Didn't the Navy help out, help you?

Mrs. Smith: Certainly not. What Navy? They had the Navy purchasing office in Shanghai, which is no more good to you than that sofa is. Not as good if you want to sit on it. There was no, no---so anyway, the next day, there we are. What to do? Very agitating. The first thing I have to do is the customs. I could leave the children aboard ship because they were 6, 8, 10 and 12. I could leave them aboard ship because they always had people, not nurses, but you know, attendants of some sort, women. I had an awful time at customs, because, you see, we had declared a gun. "No got." And the three things you couldn't bring in were salt, due to the salt cabal, because it had to do with the Boxer business.

Q: I didn't know that.

Mrs. Smith: There was a tax on salt.

Q: I see.

---

*For a firsthand account of Lieutenant Commander Smith's experiences in the Noa (DD-343) during this period, see "Nanking, March 24, 1917" (Proceedings, January 1928, pages 1-21), and "The Protection of American Nationals in China" (Proceedings, December 1930, pages 1097-1104).

Mrs. Smith: I don't know how it worked, but anyhow, you couldn't bring in salt, firearms, or obscene literature. I mean, I'd be so apt to have obscene literature traveling with four kids. I had a perfectly awful time with customs.

Q: Did they speak English?

Mrs. Smith: Well, some of them spoke pidgin. So then also I went ashore; I went to the Astor Hotel first, which is not far from the Bund.* I think I was all by myself. I don't know how I managed that; I don't remember.

Q: Weren't there any other wives with you at that point?

Mrs. Smith: Some wife must have gone with me. I don't remember who. I really don't remember who. But they were going to Manila, most of them. I don't remember. None of them got off in Shanghai but me. But I didn't want to go to Manila, and the ship was up there, you know. What would I do in Manila? It would be just the same basket. So anyhow, I went to Astor House. I couldn't afford that. Then we went to the Palace.

Q: How did you get transported from the dock to the hotel?

---

*The Bund was the waterfront area on the Whangpoo River.

Mrs. Smith: Rickshaws. Somebody must have—how did we get there? That's one of those things I don't remember. I remember being there, and I remember the Palace Hotel. They took me up and showed me this bedroom. The Palace Hotel was within walking distance of the dock where you took a boat back to the ship. See, the ship was on the other side of the river. The Palace Hotel, the bedroom they showed me—you remember those bar doors that went like this?*

Q: Yes, yes.

Mrs. Smith: In bar rooms, you know. The bedroom had doors like that.

Q: Out to the hall?

Mrs. Smith: Yes.

Q: No security, then?

Mrs. Smith: Security? No privacy, no nothing. Anyhow, so I went in and looked. And then I thought, "That's funny, what is that under the bed?" And I bent down and looked, and it was a coolie asleep under the bed. I thought, "This is the end. I

---

*The reference is to a pair of swinging doors hinged to the frame and extending to neither the top nor the bottom of the doorway.

can't do this. What will I ever do?" So I went downstairs to the desk and I said, "No. Can't. Coolie." You know.

And they said, "No, missy, no, no, missy." So I very gloomily went back to the ship. When I got there, Mrs. Clement was there, and I knew her very slightly. They were at the Academy when we were, you see, but the thing was, we lived on Southgate Avenue. We hadn't five cents, we had four children, we didn't foregather with them much. We both liked to read in the evenings, so you see, we didn't do an awful lot of running around. Today you run around. You've got a car, you go here, you go there. Then if you went, you had to walk. You don't walk all the way down to the Naval Academy for nothing, so to speak.

So Mrs. Clement said, "I tell you." Mrs. Clement has a brother who's a missionary here in Shanghai. "Let me call him up and see if he can help." So Mrs. Clement--the brother's wife--said she would come down to the dock the next day and meet me, because I had to find someplace. The ship was in there three days. I had to get off or do something. So she met me. Meanwhile, I was panicked, you may imagine. This is a story that Roy thinks is so entertaining, and I said it wouldn't happen to anybody else, I bet, but me. However, she said she knew a place that I could stay. It was really a Chinese-run boarding house, but Mrs. Doyen, the wife of the famous general during the First World War, lived there--based there, you might say. The fact that she was there meant that the young wives whose ships were up river would come and stay, and there was a room. I could go there and stay. So it was at least a start. It was out in French Town in the French concession, and so all right, we get rickshaws and she goes with me. This is panicking, too, because naturally the children were thrilled with rickshaws. The first thing I knew, I had four rickshaws and four children going off in different directions, and I didn't know what to say. I ran screaming up the street. I finally pushed two girls in a rickshaw and Roy--I forget, but anyhow, so then we went to this place, arrived on the scene. Mrs. Doyen, whom I had known--my mother, I don't think, ever knew her particularly, but knew who she was. You know, in those days it was a small Navy. You knew everybody. Anyway, she said all right, and she told me how much it would be. We had two great big rooms, and the windows looked right over a Chinese compound, and it was just as if you took the glass out of that window and had it just like that. Right underneath our window was one of those commune stinkpots that they use instead of bathrooms. Smells were terrific, and right over there is the Chinese compound, and they never go to bed in China. And the children were entranced, fascinated, you can imagine.

Q: For the time being they were, anyway.

Mrs. Smith: Wouldn't you be? Heaven sakes. I don't know if the girls were, but anyhow, Roy was all for new and interesting things. So anyway, pretty soon the number one boy came upstairs and said, "Missy, children want supper or dinner?"

I asked what the difference was. Supper was some very casual thing, not milk toast, because there wasn't any milk, but I don't know what. I don't remember what it was, but practically nothing. And Roy, at 12, was accustomed to a real dinner, you know. So I said dinner. Then he said it cost a little more. This scared me, too, because, you know, the price is going to escalate. So we go down to dinner. We're sitting around a table, and in the middle of dinner, a shooting, bang, bang, and some lady is brought in and laid on the floor. I could see her catercorner.

Q: Chinese lady?

Mrs. Smith: I don't know what kind of a lady she was. No, she wasn't, as a matter of fact; I think she was French. And Roy, of course, stuck under his seat, and I grabbed him by the seat of the pants, "Sit down, sit down, you're not going out there with a shooting." The girls, I think, the rest of them were a little nervous, but not Roy. So I made him, to his rage, stay, you see, and they brought her in. Then Mrs. Doyen warned me to be very careful not to let anybody eat anything except thus and so, well-cooked, you know, nothing raw. I don't remember if we were offered anything raw but no fruit, nothing like that. So then I regard that very agitating.

So then we went upstairs and went to bed. In Shanghai, the

mosquitos are that big—I swear to you, they are.

Q: Worse than Panama?

Mrs. Smith: Oh, yes. I've been in Panama. Oh! Panama's nothing. Nothing! Wild tigers, they were. And they descended on us in hordes. You see, the windows are just great big holes in the wall.

Q: What about bed bugs?

Mrs. Smith: I don't remember any bed bugs, no. There wouldn't have been bed bugs, I guess. But we had what you'd call an agitated night. The next day I had found what had happened was these robbers had been caught and the Annamite police chased them and they shot one, and he was hung over the wall of the house down here, and the lady had fainted from all this going on and was carried in. As far as I knew, she was dead, you see. I thought this was all pretty agitating. So then Mrs. Clement turned up and said, "What kind of a night did you have?"

And I said, "Perfectly awful. Terrible. Do you think it's going to be like this all the way?"

And she said, "Well, I have another idea for you. There is a Mr. Bernard, who's an American, and he lives out in the French concession, and his wife has gone home to do some business. And he's living there and he's looking for a housekeeper."

I said, "Look, I can't keep house in Shanghai for a strange man, for goodness sakes."

And she said, "Well, he would be glad to have you."

I said to Mrs. Doyen, "Look, is that comme il faut? Shall I go live with this gent?"

She said, "Well, you've got four children and he's got three."

I said, "Yes, but the children all go to bed early. What happens then, you might say?"

And finally I was so desperate, I said, "Okay." So he came and moved us out. And he was a nice, little fat man; he'd been out there for years and years.

Q: How old a man was he?

Mrs. Smith: Well, he was older than me, certainly. I guess Bonnie was six. He had rickshaws and stuff and took us all out. It was a big house out on the very edge of the French concession, and a wall. Everything had walls. It was pockmarked with bullets, because the Chinese territory was out that side of the road. However, that didn't worry me then. I was desperate.

Q: And we talk about the wild and wooly West.

Mrs. Smith: Yes, and people described it. I had got friends with an English gal who lived next door, and she said that when they heard the fighting, the Chinese all had umbrellas and all had tea, and if it rained, they stopped fighting. This is what the book says. The very sensible Chinese, very pragmatic--the small army could see that it was outnumbered and joins forces with the big army.

However, when we arrived on the scene, Mr. Bernard was very pleasant. He was, I suppose, maybe ten years older than me, a little fat man, and he told me he'd come out to China and sold Singer sewing machines walking through the countryside. In those days, you had cash money. You had to have a wheelbarrow for the cash.

Q: It was so inflated.

Mrs. Smith: No.

Q: You mean so big.

Mrs. Smith: And even when we were there, you went shopping for money, you know, and you got an exchange. You got so much. It was all cockeyed. You didn't get two for one. Heaven knows what you got, and I'm never good at arithmetic. When you went on the tram, you had to pay in coppers, 14 coppers. Can you imagine me on a tram with the children? I was bogged down with coppers. You could hardly move.

But anyhow, our first night there, we had a pleasant dinner, the number one boy and all the kids and everything was fine. And then we went to bed, and by this time I was pretty well exhausted. And the girls had a bedroom here, and my bed was in a little sort of hallish place in between, you see, and the boys had a bedroom there. So I fell asleep in bed.

Q: And where was the other family?

Mrs. Smith: What other family do you mean?

Q: The children and the man.

Mrs. Smith: I don't know where they slept. It was a good-sized house. I don't know where they were, somewhere around. As a matter of fact, I never thought about it. I fall asleep, and the first thing I know, my bed is being violently shaken like this, and I see little pinpoints of light up here. Mr. Bernard had told me that he was renting me a room. He'd rented me three rooms, the third one reluctantly, because he'd rented it to a young man who was out there but had gotten in a fight with a rickshaw coolie and was in the hospital with a broken hand. So I didn't know what these little points of light were, I couldn't imagine. So I sat up in bed and said, "What is that? Who are you?"

And he said, "What are you doing in my bed?"

I said, "Who are you? What have you got to do with this

anyway?"

And he said, "That's my bed. I rent it from Mr. Bernard." He'd got out of the hospital, and come back, he thought, home. He finds he had been invaded by us.

So I said, "Beat it. Beat it. Go away." So he went away. I don't know what became of him. He disappeared. And then I was exhausted again and I slept a little more, and then the bed began doing this under me. I hung over the edge, and looked, and there was a coolie underneath the bed, and all he was doing, poor thing, was he thought it was easier to get into the girls' room and get their shoes to polish, but he was creeping under the bed.

Q: To get to their room?

Mrs. Smith: To get to them. All he wanted were the shoes and my shoes and the boys' shoes, you see. I thought, "Gee, this is some session."

Well, I don't remember how long we were there, not terribly long. Meanwhile, Cam took command of the Noa up in Chefoo, and immediately ran into a typhoon, the first typhoon he'd ever known. The ship had been commanded by a classmate of his who thought it would be a good idea for Cam to take over in the middle of the typhoon, you know.* If anything happened, it wouldn't be his pigeon. So they had quite a time coming down.

---

*The commanding officer of the USS Noa (DD-343) prior to Lieutenant Commander Smith was Lieutenant Commander Alfred T. Clay, USN, who served in that capacity from 1924 to 1925.

They took green seas over the forecastle and broke out the glass in the bridge screen, some of it. Quite a time.

Q: He must have had some concern for you, too.

Mrs. Smith: I'm sure he had.

Q: In a strange city.

Mrs. Smith: In a strange city with four kids, I'm sure he did.* I went down to the Navy purchasing office and carefully left word where I was, and they said, "Yes, yes, yes."

Q: Were they reliable then?

Mrs. Smith: Didn't pay any attention at all. And they said I could send a telegram. I don't know what good that was, but anyway, I did everything they said. But I don't know how he was ever going to find me. I couldn't imagine how he was going to find me. I thought I was going to be stuck there.

Q: What about your supply of money?

---

*With Mrs. Smith were Roy Campbell III, born 14 May 1913, Mary Alger, born 22 June 1915, Louisa Taylor, born 24 April 1917, and Montgomery Meigs, born 1 April 1919.

Mrs. Smith: As I tell you, we drew a dead horse, so I had that much money, which I didn't want to spend then. I thought, "Who knows what will happen?" I had tickets to Manila and could make it to the ship.

Q: How did you carry your money, by the way? There were no travelers' checks, were there?

Mrs. Smith: Yes, we had travelers' checks. Yes, we had some sort of travelers' checks. Of course, you had to change your money when you went to Manila. There you got two for one, and you had to come back to the Shanghai American Bank and change to that, and you always lost on that. My second daughter—they kept these big silver dollars in those trays that you see that hold forks and knives, with divisions, and they do like this, abacus, and so on. I was changing my Manila money into Shanghai money, and, of course, you had Hong Kong money, Chefoo money, Shanghai money, all of it different, whatever you changed to.

Q: You lost on every change.

Mrs. Smith: Sure you did. And Lou was then, I guess eight or nine. She says, "I want cumshaw. My mother wants cumshaw."*

---
*"Cumshaw" is a slang term for obtaining something without official payment.

This was the second time we went to Chefoo, not the first time. By this time she had learned about cumshaw. She said, "My mother has spent more money in this place than any place we've ever been in. I want cumshaw. I want a dollar." But anyway, we survived.

And then one day, to my enormous relief, number one boy came upstairs and said, "Missy, one piece long master have got." Tall, he meant. Like Roy, he was just about the same height. "One piece long master have got." Boy, I fell down the stairs with excitement, you know.

Then we stayed in Shanghai, the children went to school, and they were like lepers, as far as the missionaries were concerned.

Q: Did you stay in the same place?

Mrs. Smith: I stayed with Mr. Bernard right along. He was very nice, very good.

Q: Did you get better quarters?

Mrs. Smith: No, I had the same rooms right straight through, but my visiting friend didn't come back. There was a door, but he just opened the door and came in, you see, and he just took the foot of the bed and shook it, and he was lighting a match and holding it up to see who it was. Lucky it wasn't a flashlight, it would have probably scared me to death. It was bad enough as it was. We went along there, and we were there until November. We went out in June, and we went to Japan, of course, in July. And then we were in Shanghai.

Q: Did you make some friends while you were there?

Mrs. Smith: Well, I made friends with the English lady next door, and there was one classmate of my husband's who was there with his wife, and that was one of those things where he courted the daughter and eventually married the mother, so the mother was not exactly in my age bracket, but I used to see her. You had no real opportunity. Where were you going to meet anybody? You couldn't go out and walk the streets, you know. Mr. Bernard's wife had gone. I don't remember that he knew anybody.

Q: It must have been sort of lonesome for you, then, even though you had the children to look after.

Mrs. Smith: Well, I had the kids, and I used to go out. I had to have a private rickshaw to get the children to school, and I used to go out with my rickshaw and meet Mrs. Meade and do things, or meet my English friend. We went down--speaking of the congressmen, I went down to tea with her one day at the Palace Hotel, and it was full of drunks galloping all over the place, American drunks. And I said, "Who in the name of goodness could those be?"

And she said, "Those are your congressmen." They came out on the <u>Chaumont</u>, you see.

Q: The same contingent.

Mrs. Smith: The contingent that took the ship instead of us, and they were terrible. I was ashamed to death, especially the English lady, you know. It's embarrassing. There was enough to do. I told you you don't need a great deal when you've got that many kids. As I said, we went shopping, went around, went here and there. We couldn't do very much because at that particular period, we were extremely unpopular. I had an amah for the children, and the amah and the rickshaw boy took the kids to school. It was not terribly far, because otherwise I might have been--well, you'd be walking along the street and some Chinaman would come spit in your face. You know, like that. And it was really not safe. You couldn't go running around by yourself. You really couldn't do very much. It was a bit unnerving. And one warlord had the city, and you could tell, because the uniforms are green and then another day go out and another warlord had the city and the uniforms were brown.

Q: How confusing.

Mrs. Smith: Also entertaining. How do you know what they're going to do?

Q: What side, yes. The school was run by what?

Mrs. Smith: It was run by businessmen and missionaries.

Q: The Americans?

Mrs. Smith: Yes, Americans. It was the American Shanghai School. It was in the French concession. There was a French concession and a British concession.

Q: Yes.

Mrs. Smith: No American concession, no. And one day I went down the street, and then, of course, the ship's—Mrs. Tobin, her husband was the exec, she was there, too.* I mean, she was living in Shanghai, but she had been living there for some time, and I don't know where she was living. They could afford to live in a hotel, you see, but I couldn't, goodness knows. So I was necessarily to myself to some extent. But we went shopping one time. She knew a nice silk shop, so we went, and I went first to the hotel and picked her up, and then we went—it's a marvelous

---

*Mrs. Robert G. Tobin.

feeling to go around in a rickshaw. At first you think, "This is terrible." But then the rickshaw coolies were so gay and merry and laughing and talking, seemed to suffer no pain, seemed to enjoy themselves, so that you stopped feeling sorry for them, really, you know, except in your mind. But anyway, we went to this place off Nanking Road, went along a big road, and we turned off into a narrow road like this and stopped. She had asked the hotel--I didn't know, I had hardly been there a few days--she asked the hotel how much to pay, you see, and of course, if you pay too much, they think you're so rich, you can pay more. If you pay too little, they scream again, so you can't win. So we put the amount of money, they wouldn't take it. We put the amount of money the hotel told us on the floor of the rickshaw. We went into this silk shop and hoped for the best. We finished our purchases, and we thought, "Well, we don't want to go out that way, we'll go the other way." You see, the street was so. This is Nanking Road and this is--I forget, another big road, I forget which. I mean, they were not little narrow ones like the crack we were in. So we went there, and lo and behold, our coolies had outsmarted us. They were there. And they fell upon us. We each had a rickshaw coolie, of course, and they each had a couple of followers, I suppose. They began screaming and yelling and holding up their hands, "Money, money, money," and threatening us, you know, like this. They didn't actually hit us, but she had an umbrella in her hand and one snatched her umbrella and threatened her with it, you see. And frankly, we were scared pink. There wasn't one soul to be seen except a sea of Chinese, and here we are in the middle of them. Would you like it?

Q: Knowing that Americans were unpopular.

Mrs. Smith: Oh, we were very unpopular. We were snakes in the grass. The idea was Americans were all right and British were unpopular, but the coolies couldn't tell the difference between us, could they? And before I got off the ship, one of the ship's officers had been ashore the night before and got beaten up. I mean, before I left the Dollar boat, which didn't give you any sense of confidence.* Apparently he got in a rickshaw and they ran off with him goodness knows where and beat him up.

Q: And sometimes they went beyond that and killed them, didn't they?

Mrs. Smith: Yes, but they weren't killing them so freely in those days. But you really couldn't go running around. Anyway, here they are, and they really scared us pink. We didn't know what was going to happen. And what we did was, we just walked as fast as we possibly could, there was a bigger highway at the end of the street. If we could make that, we thought we'd be better

---
*The Dollar Line was then a U.S.-flag shipping line.

off. There might be a street policeman or something. And then we suddenly discovered an old Chinese gentleman all dressed in gray silk.

Q: A mandarin type?

Mrs. Smith: Well, you know, long gray silk gown and a black . . .

Q: Scholar type.

Mrs. Smith: They all wore fedora hats, no matter what else, and we rushed up to him. He couldn't speak any more English than we could speak Chinese, but he saw what we were confronted with, you see, totally surrounded with, and we talked to him in pidgin, and the crowd sort of fell back a little. He didn't actually do anything or say anything, but it fell back a little, so we escaped down to the main road, got another rickshaw and went home. And I told Mr. Bernard about that, and he said, "You absolutely must report this to the police. Otherwise, this kind of thing, attacking foreigners in the British concession [where we were, you see, not where we were living, but where we were shopping], you must go to court and do it." Well, we were scared to death to do that. We thought this coolie will catch up with us sometime, you know, and get even. So we appeared in the mixed court. I've been trying to think ever since. There were three judges, a French judge, a British judge, and an American judge, and I don't remember if there were two at a time or three. I think there were two. I think there was a British and an American, I'm not sure, but they sat in what they called a mixed court, you see. The judges in different categories. There may have been three; I don't remember. So we had to stand up and give our testimony, and they dragged this poor thing away.

Q: They had the . . .

Mrs. Smith: They had somebody. I don't know where they had gotten him. I don't know anything about it. I just followed what Mr. Bernard told us to do, you see. And then they said they'd put him in the clink for a month and then, of course, Caroline and I thought, "Lord, if he gets out and maybe tracks us down, what will we do?" It was bad enough having the kids go to school. Sort of nerve-racking.

Q: What about your purchases on that occasion? Did you lose them?

Mrs. Smith: No, no, we carried them under our arm. They didn't want those; they wanted money.

Q: They didn't want the silk that you bought.

Mrs. Smith: Well, they didn't touch us, didn't actually touch us. They only surrounded us, screaming and yelling. The same thing happened in Chefoo when the two girls had two dolls, the kind of dolls that open and shut their eyes. And we were walking along the Bund. Chefoo was a peaceful place, really, not a big city in those days. And they were holding their dolls, you know, and talking about them, I guess. Some coolie came over to look, and another one came, and another one came, and they held up their hands, the girls held their dolls, you know, they wanted to hold them. And meanwhile, of course, we were yelling, "Chela," which means "beat it," you know. That was all we could say. And the only thing we could do was what we did before, just sternly proceed. I was a little undone by this, you might say. By this time I had gotten fairly tough.

Q: Experienced.

Mrs. Smith: Yes. I mean, if anything is exciting, out of the way, you see, you are surrounded. They were all perfectly amiable and curious, that's all, just curious, but the girls felt that if they handed out their dolls, they might never see them back, and they said they didn't want their dirty paws to touch them. But you were not free to go running around and feel easy about it, because you never knew what might happen. It might be very unpleasant, it might not. But that was after there was an incident with the British, I think, the year before, 1924. Somebody blew up the police station on Nanking Road. I don't know what happened, but anyhow it stirred things up. The Sikh policemen would, if any coolie transgressed the road, you know, stepped out of line crossing the street, the Sikh would go crack him on the head without turning a hair, and he'd fall in the gutter, and they'd leave him. I had to go up to the hospital...

Q: Life is cheap.

Mrs. Smith: Very cheap. Nobody cared. Nobody cared, and if you rescued anybody--we were at the beach swimming one time, and there was a boat over here, you know, and some man fell overboard and nobody rescued him; nobody made any effort. By this time in Chefoo, we stayed in a Russian boarding house, and I asked Mrs. Weinglass about that, and she said, "If you rescue a man, then he's your dependent for the rest of his life and your life, too. You've got to look out for him forever." So you're a little cautious how you rescue people, especially if they're a coolie, just lie back and there you are, you know.

Q: And you have to feed him forevermore.

Mrs. Smith: You have to feed him, take care of him for the rest of your life. He's it. So it's a very suspicious life.

Q: My!

Mrs. Smith: Well, it's the kind of thing you think about it afterwards and you think, "Dear me." Well, you know, at the time it was frightening, but it was also very exciting and fun and interesting. It really was very interesting. I found China fascinating and so colorful, and the poor downtrodden ones. I was going to tell you, on the way to the hospital, my Monty, my youngest son, who was six, said that his eye bothered him, and I thought, well, I'd take him up to the hospital. And the doctor there was Chinese, and he looked him all over, and he looked at Monty, who was, after all, no fool. He was, I guess, almost seven. The doctor looked at us, at Monty, at me, and he said, "In a few months, this child will be blind in one eye, and in a year he'll be totally blind in both eyes." Now, it's very difficult to maintain sufficient expression to reassure your young when you have anybody say that to you. Bang, you know. And I didn't want Monty to--he took it all in, and it upset him for years, I mean, it really did.

Q: Well, it must have been upsetting for you, too.

Navy Wives - 165
Smith #1 - 102

Mrs. Smith: It upset me like hell, I'll tell you. It did. And so then he said that he had ...

Q: Glaucoma, was it?

Mrs. Smith: Not glaucoma, no. What he turned out to have was, he had a partly atrophied nerve in one eye, which nothing ever happened about, but at the same time, it was all that I could do at that time, and the doctor said that the children undoubtedly had trachoma, because it would be impossible not to pick it up. So then I had to take them--not Roy, he was on the ship, I guess.

Q: That's in the muscles, isn't it?

Mrs. Smith: Trachoma is a filth disease.

Q: From pork, isn't it?

Mrs. Smith: No, I think it's...

Q: Trichinosis?

Mrs. Smith: No, I think it's an infection. No, it's how you handle the rickshaw hurts your eye.

Q: I see.

Mrs. Smith: You know you're not going to make the children wash their hands every two seconds. They didn't have it, thank God. Of course, this was alarming because I thought, "You can't go back into the United States with it. How will I get home?" I'm only telling you the alarming spots. I'm not telling you all the good spots.

Q: They add up to something quite impressive, I must say.

Mrs. Smith: They do? They were quite exciting, they really were. But anyway, on the way up to the hospital, I said to the doctor, "Poor thing, this man out here, you know, lying here, an old man, coughing right beside him." It's not good luck to die in the house, so they would put you out on the sidewalk, you know, have your coffin, handy and you'd die. They put you in, and that's it. Of course, the coffins are all sitting above ground, you know. There was a cemetery not far from where we lived, and all these coffins are just sitting around.

Q: On top of the ground?

Mrs. Smith: Yes.

Q: Why was that?

Mrs. Smith: Don't ask me. I don't know why. That's the way it was. And, of course, some of the older ones sort of disintegrated after a while if you went and prowled, which I never did. And when we were in Baguio, Roy was going to school in Baguio, and the boys used to go on hikes, and they had burial caves and they buried their people sitting up. And to my utter horror...

Q: Sans coffin?

Mrs. Smith: No coffin. To my horror, when Roy came back from Baguio, we were going up to China in the spring, and I found my best evening dress--you could buy French clothes in Shanghai, very cheap. It looked very odd. I looked at it and in it were two horrible bones. Roy had filched them out of the burial caves. All the boys took a couple of bones as souvenirs. He had hidden them in my best dress. I said, "What do you think the customs will say?"

Q: In your couturier gown.

Mrs. Smith: Two big long leg bones. But in China, I mean, little things like that, I don't remember seeing any bones lying around, but if you had gone prowling, you probably could have found them if you had wanted to. I don't know, but life was very cheap. Very cheap. And in Chefoo, they still had a burial, a baby tower. It was not used, I think. If you had a girl baby, you went and dropped it down the tower, but the Catholic sisters established a large place there, and they took the babies.

Q: They had an orphanage.

Mrs. Smith: Well, what they had was a workshop, really. They took them and raised them up, and as soon as they were old enough to hold a needle, they taught them to do beautiful embroidery and they sew wonderful embroidered linens, you see, which was good all around. I don't know whatever happened to the girls in the end.

Q: Their eyes gave out after a while?

Mrs. Smith: Well, I don't know. They probably got married. I don't know what they did. But I mean, nobody thought anything about people dying. It was just par for the course. What do you expect? I think there's a lot in that point of view. I think people who spend their life worrying about what's going to happen then, when they're going to die, and you spend your life with a doctor trying to preserve it.

Q: It certainly does illustrate the difference between the East and the West.

Mrs. Smith: It's the most enormous difference. And I got undone with the missionaries for life because there were all these different groups, and I admired the Catholic ones, because the nuns went out and stayed, and they had schools and they trained the children. They did this, you know. But the others, it was a joke. When we got back, people would joke about it and say, "Well, the missionaries write home and say, 'With the few remaining bricks after the church, we built the house.'" Well, they lived in nice big houses with plenty of servants and plenty of food. Of course, their missionary pay was big out there.

Q: They lived in compounds, didn't they?

Mrs. Smith: Well, everybody had compounds to some extent, you know, even though it was only a bamboo thing. And we didn't have anything to do with them because they wouldn't have anything to do with us. We might just as well have been lepers. Supposing we say here are the Baptists, and here we say the Episcopalians, here we say somebody else is, and here they are in a country that was civilized thousands of years before any of us knew what anything was but in caves. Here they are telling them, "I say my God is right and you must follow this. I say this, and I say this." And as he says in his book, how the Chinese––they have a million gods themselves. How are you going to pick out which one of ours we all say this is the only one? It's so stupid.

Q: Now, the British missionaries were somewhat different, weren't they? They established hospitals. They went in for the medical side of things to improve the situation.

Mrs. Smith: Well, the only hospital I had anything to do with––I had something to do with the one in Shanghai because my daughter broke her arm, and that was fierce, too, because I had taken the children––there wasn't very much to do there, you know. I had taken the Bernard children and my children down to this sort of girl guide thing, you know. And there they had a slide like this, and my younger daughter slid down it and fell off and broke her arm. She had broken her other arm two years before, at home, and she broke her elbow before, which is bad. It got all right, but she was very young and it healed. This time I didn't know, it seemed to be in here. And there I was. There wasn't a soul I had ever seen in my entire life at the girl guide thing, except, you know, and I was responsible for seven children. And more people came and said, "Can I help you? Is there anything I can do for you?"

And I said, "Yes, tell me the name of the best hospital in Shanghai." And they'd sort of sheer off.

And finally some man came up to me and said, "The Shanghai General Hospital is the best one." And he said, "Can I do anything for you?"

And I said, "Yes, you certainly can. You can take all these children home. I don't want to take them to the hospital with me." So he took them all off with him in a car. He had a car. So I got a rickshaw and took poor Lou to the hospital. It was race week, and again we were as popular as lepers. It was run by sisters, nuns, and a more cold-hearted bunch I never met, in my opinion. Anyhow, they put Lou in a room and said, "Of course, you won't have a doctor until--you better take her home."

I said, "I can't take her way out there in a rickshaw, bumping along and bring her back." They said next week, or three days, or four days, whatever it was. I said, "I can't do that." I raised the roof. Wouldn't you?

So anyway, they put her in a room and said, "We'll keep her here if you like."

Meanwhile, I began getting cold chills. "What have I done with the children? Where did they go? How do I know who took them? How do I know they took them home?" My only hope was he wouldn't do much, there were six of them, he couldn't do much with six of them, but still, how did you know in this country where all sorts of things went on?

So anyway, they said I couldn't have anything done about her arm, so I went fiercely down and stationed myself in the front hall, whatever it was, and in comes a man who looked like a doctor, and I fell upon him. It turns out, fortunately for me, he's a bone fellow, he's coming entirely out of context...

Q: Just the right doctor.

Mrs. Smith: Yes. He's out of context entirely. He's coming to see a patient.

Q: That's what you call Navy luck.

Mrs. Smith: Yes. So I fell upon him like mad, and after I had made enough noise, he said, all right, he would set her arm the next day if I would find somebody to give her anesthetic. Me! So I madly sent a message out to the ship—not my husband's ship, because my husband's ship wasn't even there. I sent it to the flagship, and I got a message back from the dotor saying he hadn't given an anesthetic in years; he really couldn't undertake it. So in the end, the surgeon finally found one. He told me, well, he would if I couldn't get one. Imagine, where was I going to get one? So I said—my little girl, after all, was only eight, and she'd broke her other arm two years ago and had a bad time with it, and she's trying very hard to be brave. She said, "I'm trying not to cry. I'm trying very hard to be brave."

And I said, "Would you let me walk with her as far as the

operating room door?" You know, just to give her that much confidence.

And he said, "Yes, of course, perfectly all right."

So that night they let me stay in the hospital with her that night, having telephoned home and found the kids were all there. And the next morning they came to get her and put her on the tray, and carted her off, and I started along beside her, holding her hand, and the nun says, "Go back. You can't come."

I said, "The doctor said I could."

She said, "No." She said, "After all, this is Sunday. We don't usually do anything on this day. It's a great concession for doing it. And if you come any closer, we'll take her back to bed."

So off the poor little lamb went by herself, and they set her arm, brought her back, and I said to the nun, "Was it a bad break, or what?"

And the nun said, "Well, of course, the X-ray man won't work. This is race week. He won't work for a couple of days. And if her arm is not set properly, of course, you understand, they'll have to rebreak it and begin again."

So I think, well, maybe I've done terrible things, you know. However, fortunately, he came the next day, and the X-ray man came the day after, I guess, and it was set all right. Then I sashayed between home and Shanghai General Hospital. But it was the Shanghai General Hospital, I think it was run by business people, probably Americans and British both. It was in the British concession. I don't know who ran it, I really don't. And as for British hospitals, there may have been some, I don't know. I never saw any.

Interview Number 2 with Mrs. Mary Smith

Place: Mrs. Smith's son's residence in Annapolis, Maryland

Date: Monday, 23 October 1978

Subject: Biography

Interviewer: John T. Mason, Jr.

Q: Mrs. Smith, last time, when you concluded, you were winding up the tour of duty in China. This was in 1928, I believe.

Mrs. Smith: We went out in June of '25, and we came back in February or March '28.

Q: Yes. So do you want to resume the story at that point?

Mrs. Smith: Well, after that, after all, then we had duty at the Torpedo Station.

Q: Up in Newport, Rhode Island.

Mrs. Smith: Newport, Rhode Island.

Q: Tell me about that. Tell me about Newport life in that time.

Mrs. Smith: Well, of course, you must remember that we'd been traveling around for three years, and I'd been traveling around with four children for three years, and going from Manila to

Chefoo every summer. We stopped in Shanghai when we got there. I couldn't afford to stay in Japan like some of the others. Then we went down to Manila, and every spring we had to go up. We had Admiral Clarence Williams, who wouldn't allow you to travel in a transport, so you had to pay your way.* It was very expensive, and this is how Roy got to Nanking, because we couldn't afford to take him up. He goes in his father's ship and I was to meet him. Then, of course, they had the fracas and he gets sent back to me, and it's terribly expensive.** So we came home, and we hadn't been there very long before my two girls said to me, "Look here, we've been here a long time, almost a month. Isn't it time we moved?"

I said, "No, it ain't. It's the first time the trunks have been unpacked in years." And it was great fun, and it was after the excitements of China where you never quite knew what was going to happen. I mean, you'd have one general take the city and one day you'd have green uniforms, and one day you'd have brown uniforms. And it's true we lived in the French concession, which was not ...

Q: Which was guarded, was it not?

---

*Admiral Clarence S. Williams, USN, Commander in Chief Asiatic Fleet.
**For an account of the "fracas" involving the ship commanded by Mrs. Smith's husband, see "U.S.S. Noa and the fall of Nanking," U.S. Naval Institute Proceedings, November 1955, pages 1221-1228.

Mrs. Smith: You wouldn't know it was guarded. You went downtown in your rickshaw, went to and from the English to French, and so on. But we were not any more popular than nothing. And the missionaries couldn't stand us. The missionaries kept pointing out that if we weren't there, things would be peaceful and lovely. It was our fault, and Roy was terribly upset because his father said to him--they were going to the Shanghai American School, which is run by missionaries and businessmen, and I had to have an amah take the girls to school, and I guess young Monty was six. He went with them, too, I guess. But his father said to Roy, "Now, if you like, you can take two friends down aboard ship. I'll be home for the weekend. You can go down and stay in my cabin. You can have movies and be aboard ship." To Roy, age 12, a weekend on the ship was just heavenly. So he asked two friends, first one and the other and their families, to his horror, just carried on as if he'd asked them to visit hell. They wouldn't think of it. Terrible! But then, I mean, all this, you never quite knew what was going to happen, who was going to get what. The ship was usually out and we were left on our own, you might say, or where you were going.

So when we got back, I thought it was lovely and peaceful. The Torpedo Station is on an island, and there were seven houses at the end, tennis courts, and a ferry which came every 20 minutes. Admiral Hart was aboard, and Admiral Hart was terribly cross then because of his dearly beloved--what was his boy's name?*

Q: There was Tommy and Roswell.

Mrs. Smith: Tommy was a friend of my younger son.

Q: Roswell.

Mrs. Smith: Roswell was infuriating, because Ross, who wouldn't do anything at school, and didn't want to go to the Naval Academy, and my Roy, our Roy, was going to Severn.** And Admiral Hart, in the evening, they used to come out and walk around the island. We all used to do that sometimes in the summer and stop on porches, you know, in the Southern style. And he was always saying things about Roswell. Roswell wouldn't do this, Roswell wouldn't do that. I gather Roswell was a carefree lad and was going to Hotchkiss School and not Severn. So as far as I was concerned, it was lovely and peaceful. I adored it over there. The kids had a dreadful time in school. They kept saying, "People say that travel is good, it teaches you, but our teachers don't know that. They say, 'Didn't you have this in arithmetic? Didn't you have that in grammar?' And we say, 'No.'" Because

---
*From 1927 to 1929, Captain Thomas C. Hart, USN, was stationed at Newport, Rhode Island, as chief ordnance inspector in charge of the torpedo station.
**Severn School in Severna Park, Maryland, a suburb of Annapolis, was an unofficial preparatory school for the service academies until the early 1970s.

over there, they went to a convent in Chefoo, which is the best we could do, and went to school in Manila, which was the best we could do, but I don't know what they learned. However, they did.

So anyway, here we got here and it was all very nice, and, as I said, my husband was—it's funny, we moved into the house that he had lived in when he was seven or eight. His father had the same duty and the same house. It hadn't changed a crumb. So it felt like old home week to him. And he rushed down below right off to see if—of course, this was Prohibition—to see if the cellar still had the racks to keep bottles in, you know, because his father ran the wine mess for the seven houses. And there were racks but no bottles, very disappointing. So then we were there, and all of a sudden we were there three years. And then he was ordered to the Memphis, which was the Special Service Squadron. And then he was ordered there in, I think, March, something like that, which was a problem about school, so we came here.

Q: Before you tell me about that tour of duty, tell me more about the life in Newport. I mean, when you were there for the three years, what sort of social life did you have?

Mrs. Smith: As far as we were concerned, of course, we arrived on the scene and there were a number of classmates and old friends. But if you lived—you had to take the ferry to and fro. The last ferry went at 11:00 o'clock, and you could have it wait for you, but you weren't popular doing that. And neither of us played bridge, and all our friends called up and said, "Come and have dinner, come and do this, what do you play?" Well, I played mah-jongg. We both learned to play that in the East, and didn't play anything else. They'd say, "Do you play bridge?" No, but we decided between us we've got to play poker. He knew how to play poker. It gave him a little nervous feeling, me learning to play poker, but that's what we did.

Q: Mah-jongg was popular, too, wasn't it?

Mrs. Smith: Yes, but not--I used to play mah-jongg all the time with the gals I've known in China. Yes, some girls I've known here. But the men didn't play very much. We used to play, go ashore and play at 11:00 o'clock and played 'til about 5:00. It was wonderful. But otherwise, we didn't. I had a terrible time because I was not taking the liquor in those days, and they'd say, "Now what will you drink?" Of course, naturally, my dear husband would drink whatever they offered him, like most naval officers.

And I said, "Nothing, thank you."

And they would have a fit and say, "You must have something."

I'd say, "No, no, I'm not thirsty."

"It doesn't make any difference; you must have something." This got to be terrible, you know. Then they started saying, "What will we give Mary to drink?" And they'd say, "I suppose, of course, she wouldn't dare touch our bathtub gin or this or that. She's afraid of us." And it got to that it got nerve-racking for me, you know.

So I said, "All right." So I began drinking. I said, well, I'd drink whatever they passed for bourbon, and I just drank it neat, you know. I found this didn't work so hot at poker because first thing you know, your glass is filled up. So that is the only reason in the world I took to drinking bourbon. But we did a lot of playing poker. We didn't go in for cocktail parties because it was forbidden.

Q: Yes.

Mrs. Smith: And we couldn't have anything to drink on the island. If you had a dinner party, which we did quite often, then you had to go ashore and have drinks at somebody else's house.

Q: And then come back on the ferry?

Mrs. Smith: And then come back on the ferry for dinner.

Q: Could you have wine at dinner?

Mrs. Smith: No. Forbidden. No, no. We were on duty with dear old Hart, who was busy telling me that his wife--what happened to

Roy in the end, that any naval officer's son should understand discipline. And there was no excuse if they didn't. And I saw him somewhere or other before Roy went into the Academy, and he resented every Navy boy that went into the Academy because Roswell didn't. And Tommy did, and Tommy used to talk to my Monty quite freely, you know.* And then when he was there, it's true what he said, you know, he said, "The Superintendent is awfully tough."**

He said, "Huh. Try him as a father."

But we had lots of that kind of thing, but cocktail parties, no. You couldn't have any drinks anyhow, and probably somebody had gone blind with the stuff that you had to buy. And I don't remember. We had, of course, in those days, it was the War College, the Torpedo Station, and Fort Adams. And during the year, there were three big dances, and everybody went out to dinner and dance. Believe it or not, people came in white tie and tails.

Q: These were formal, quite formal.

Mrs. Smith: They were formal. And can you imagine now inviting anybody to dinner and have them call up to your house and saying, "Would a white tie and tuxedo do?" Can you feature? Today they're liable to say, "Would a bathing suit do?" We had those

---
*Midshipman Thomas C. Hart, USN, Naval Academy class of 1939.
**As a rear admiral, Hart was Superintendent of the Naval Academy from 1931 to 1934.

three big festivities and then, of course, the other gals and I cooked up the Navy Junior assemblies come Christmas. There was nothing going on for the girls and boys of that in-between age, you see. Mary was ten when we went to China, so then she was 14, I guess, just about 14 or 15, along in there, and the Hewitts were there and the Draemels were there, and I forget all the other people who had daughters, and some of them had sons.* We cooked up these parties, which we had two of. I guess we had one at Christmas, and we had a terrible time because we had to make a rule "there can't be any older than or any younger than," because the girls said they didn't want any 16, 17-year-olds coming in and cutting them out. Neither did they want any baby child boys in there. So we had to be very selective. And we got in terrible trouble because they'd call up and say, "My daughter ought to be included."

We said, "No, no..."

Q: Six days before the ...

Mrs. Smith: Yes. But those, we had those, and that was fun. And otherwise, my husband played golf and I went swimming, and we didn't have to do all that calling.

Then we left there and went to Panama, and he was in the Special Service Squadron.

---

*Commander and Mrs. H. Kent Hewitt; Commander and Mrs. Milo F. Draemel.

Q: Did you mix any with the local people up there?

Mrs. Smith: Yes, we did, to some extent. We did. Because my husband and I always liked to know other people besides just Navy. We did, and what did we use to do? I've forgotten. I guess we belonged to the art association, used to go to meetings there or something. And of course, you see, my mother-in-law was Miss Sampson and grew up there.* The admiral was there on duty, I guess, twice. And she grew up there as a girl, and she knew all kinds of people, you know, naturally older than us, but they were some contemporaries of ours around we knew through her. And she would have liked me to have done a lot more going around and calling on older people, becoming acquainted with the elite, but after all, there is a busy life. I mean, getting the kids outfitted and oriented; they had a terrible time with their lessons at first, you know, until they got fixed, and loved to go swimming, and we liked to play golf, so we used to do that whenever we had a spare moment. And we both loved to read, so we spent a lot of time peacefully, you might say. We didn't feel we had to run, but we played poker almost every Saturday, I should say, and went to parties in between. It was quite gay.

Q: What was a dinner party like? I mean, what kind of entertainment did you have at a dinner party?

---
*Mrs. Smith's mother-in-law was Margaret Aldrich Sampson, daughter of the Superintendent of the Naval Academy from 1886 to 1890. She married Lieutenant Roy C. Smith, Sr., USN, in 1887.

Mrs. Smith: You had conversation, my dear sir. Period.

Q: You went off the island and had cocktails somewhere.

Mrs. Smith: Well, you'd go to somebody's house and have a drink, and come back and have dinner.

Q: And then?

Mrs. Smith: After dinner, you simply sat and talked.

Q: Mixed group, or did the men separate from the women?

Mrs. Smith: No, of course not. That's country style. No, that's farmer stuff. No, certainly not. They were civilized. They sat around. No, we sat around all together and talked. And you didn't stay until 3:00 o'clock in the morning, for goodness sakes. I mean, if you had dinner, we'll say, at 7:00, and then by, say, 10:00, around there, everybody went home.

Q: How big a dinner party would you have? How many guests would you have? What kind of help did you have?

Mrs. Smith: Well, everybody had a cook in those days. That's one of my difficulties. I couldn't imagine ever not having a servant in the house, so I never did learn all the proper arts I should know, the domestic arts, because we had duty away, you know, and when we got to Newport, the woman who used to be my nurse or cook or something in Annapolis, her daughter married a sailor, so she was there. She saw our name in the paper, so she rushed over, and I had her.

Q: She was the cook?

Mrs. Smith: She was the cook, and she cooked and served, both, as I remember. Mostly we had eight or possibly ten. The only time we went to 12, we had the Harts. And naturally I wished to be very stylish. I guess we had a woman come in and serve, just serve. And this gal came over and said she could serve, she was fine, and I thought, well, she's pretty good. So she came over on the ferry just in time to serve dinner, and it was a new one. I didn't like her looks much. Oh, yes, she knew everything. Fine, all right. I couldn't do anything then. So we had soup, that was all right. And then she opened the door, the pantry door, swinging door, put her head in, and said to me--no, I guess we had a fruit cup or something first, she opens the door, put her head in and said, "Y'all want soup?" I nearly died. Today I'm old and tough and I would have laughed, but in those days I nearly perished! Can you imagine? So then I said, "Yes." So she brought in this soup, and then she came to take the soup plates off. I kept hissing at her, you know, and she came off and she started to take the plates and stacked them to carry off two or three at once. I almost perished. It was awful. But you could get perfectly civilized service without any trouble, really and truly, I mean, you could. And we didn't have the elaborate dinners. I remember the dinner parties my mother used to have where you had two or three wines, and you had a soup, you had something first, then had a soup, an entree, you had fish, and you had a roast, chicken, beef, something, then a salad, and dessert. Then the women separated from the men. In our day they didn't. Houses weren't big enough, in most cases. You rented a house in town with no place to separate to. No, but it was all very informal and great fun, and we knew people in town, not a great many. We met some people in St. George's, which is quite starchy, a little enclave, even now, you know what I mean.

Q: The church, you mean?

Mrs. Smith: No, St. George's School.

Q: Oh, the school.

Mrs. Smith: Not the church, the school. It's quite a little thing, you know, and I think they belong together. And of course, in our day, really, there was the Navy and the Army, because there was Fort Adams. And then, I don't remember any Marines to speak of. There was a Marine barracks. No, that was here. No, there were no Marines. I don't remember. But then there were, of course, the Bellevue Avenue crowd, who were very to themselves, and you couldn't play around with them very well, and you know some.*

Q: They were only there in the summertime, anyway, weren't they?

Mrs. Smith: Yes, that's right. And then there were the old-time Newporters whose roots had been there when islanders started, and then, of course, there were the tradespeople. And these groups, it's so today, the fringes mesh, but not too much, you know what I mean. Because, after all, I think the people on the avenue have a feeling that money is the thing, and they are apt to be if you go to Bailey's Beach for lunch, as I have on various occasions--they are surprised if you know anybody. I had two or three very good friends I used to play cards with. After I learned to play Bolivia, we used to play that a lot. But ordinarily, you don't, because you can't run around with people who have millions of dollars. Their whole point of view is different.

Q: Yes.

Mrs. Smith: Unless you want to be, and there have been cases when we were there, a naval officer--I've forgotten his name, and his wife were sort of proteges of the princes or whoever it was.

―――――――――
*The mansions of the very rich were on Bellevue Avenue.

But unless you want to do that--but we met, I remember, one couple we liked very much at St. George's, thought they were very pleasant, and I said to her that we would like to see more of them, would they come and see us. Because in those days at the Torpedo Station, the band played in the afternoon. Was it a band or music? I tell you what, we had a day at home once a week. Everybody on the island had a day at home, and there was music then. And it was all very gay and nice, and I asked her to come. And she said to me, "Well, you know, it's hardly worthwhile getting to know you Navy people because you're gone before you get anywhere." Now, that point of view--I don't know if it exists now, but it was in the air.

Q: It's a very valid point of view, of course.

Mrs. Smith: Well, up to a point. But good night, are you going to say you won't enjoy a rose because you might have a lily the next day? Not that I'm comparing ourselves with roses and lilies, but I mean, all right, are you not going to eat an oyster because tomorrow you might have crab? I don't see the point. It's discouraging if they meet you like that. But we saw quite a few, but mostly there were so many old friends and classmates, that you didn't sashay outside. I guess that was when the Kalbfuses were there, I'm not sure.* Admiral Kalbfus, I

---

*Rear Admiral Edward C. Kalbfus, USN, was president of the Naval War College from June 1939 to November 1942.

remember, when he ...

Q: He was at the War College.

Mrs. Smith: He was president of the War College. I guess that was when we came back, I've forgotten, because then we went to Panama and came back from Panama to the War College. That was in '33-'34.

Q: That's probably when Kalbfus was there.

Mrs. Smith: What's when Kalbfus was there. Because I remember when Mrs. Kalbfus was Miss Brown, because my father was head of the department of mechanics, and we lived, as I said, in Sampson Row; we were the first people to move into the house.* The first thing that happened was they came around and said, "The porch is cracking off from the house." It was all made ground, you know. I remember my mother having screaming fits and me thinking, "That would be fun, lovely, if the porch all fell off." It impressed me that way. And then Mr. Roosevelt decided that it was ridiculous for midshipmen to spend so much time with their noses in books. Absurd, they should have more seamanship, more of that kind of thing.

---

*This reference is to Mrs. Smith's time at the Naval Academy in the first decade of the 20th century.

Q: More activity.

Mrs. Smith: That's right. So they did away with mechanics and Stimson Brown, who was Mrs. Kalbfus's father, was moved over and took our house and took that job, and my father was then on duty.* As I said, he was on duty the whole time at the ordnance board in Washington. But he also was secretary-treasurer of the Institute, so it was a question of would we live in Washington or here. And Ma decided on here. But I remember perfectly well when Miss Brown was being courted by Kalbfus. I don't mean I saw them, but I mean, you know, you hear these things in the air around you; you don't care much. It's funny, when you think back, you remember a phrase or an item or something and it has no context in time. I mean, I can remember perfectly well being here, but how I got there, why I went there, I don't remember at all. I have friends who remember the whole darn thing, down to the train they took and the time and everything. But I don't. I remember it in spots. You remember, for instance, something that the family said or talked about that you didn't really care but just sort of, you just heard it. And I remember when Miss Brown married Kalbfus, so he was at the college. And then we had a terrific time because--talk about social! He insisted that everybody call on everybody on the staff. I mean, every staff person call. First he moved the college plane, and that year was

---
*Captain Stimson J. Brown, USN, professor of mathematics at the Naval Academy from 1901 to 1912.

a wild year. We had just got home from Panama, and my daughter, my other daughter had had one of those quiet, off-the-record marriages, you might say, which gave everybody 900 fits, you know. And then Roy got himself out of the Naval Academy for demerits, which nearly killed everybody, and my youngest son had appendicitis, and we were living in an apartment on the second floor, the furnace was coal, and on the second floor, the furnace, stove, everything on the second floor. And here's my daughter home with a new baby, and she was very young. Monty had appendicitis, my husband was in the hospital with high blood pressure, and I'm running the furnace. It was what you might call a busy winter. Everybody said to me, "Why didn't you have high blood pressure?"

I said, "I haven't got time; I'm too busy." So that winter was a blank, as far as anything social is concerned.

And the second winter, he was on the staff, and Admiral Kalbfus required we call on every single person there. Thank God, it was not like now when they've got hundreds of them and they've got all kinds of representatives from the countries that you can't imagine have a navy. Iran, for instance—has it got a Navy? I don't know about Iran, but all kinds of crazy countries. But we had to call on them all, which was a terrible chore because Pa was dying to go out and play golf, and in the winter, you know, in those days...

Q: Were these evening calls?

Mrs. Smith: No, no. We had to go on formal calling in the afternoon.

Q: Late afternoon?

Mrs. Smith: Well, you couldn't go before he got home from the College, so you started out at 4:00 o'clock. And half past 5:00 was the latest time. Everybody had a cook. It wasn't like now when the lady of the house is scrambling to get dinner. But at the same time, when I think about it, 15 minutes was the--you could allow 15 minutes for a call.

Q: Only 15 minutes?

Mrs. Smith: That was long enough. That was polite. And nobody offered you a drink, for God's sake. Nobody ever heard of such a thing as a drink.

Q: Not even tea?

Mrs. Smith: Well, some of them would offer you tea, but you knew perfectly well if you accepted tea, it took a long time, and if you allowed yourself six calls in the afternoon, you wanted to get them wiped off. You didn't want to stick around there and have tea. Do you?

Q: So what was the purpose of a call like that?

Mrs. Smith: It wasn't so bad, really. Now they have one great big mishmash party, to which everybody goes. The idea was, that way you got to some extent acquainted. I mean, for instance, you called on the Browns and you liked the Browns, you thought they were very attractive, and you're the old-timer, so you ask them to come and see you. You make friends with them.

Q: In 15 minutes.

Mrs. Smith: Well, you can tell in 15 minutes if you think you're going to like them, can't you? Some people in five minutes you know you're not going to like them. You're surely as smart as that. You know that perfectly well. Well, all right, you could stay more; you could stay half an hour. You could stay as long as you wanted. You could stay all afternoon. Sometimes you weakened and had tea, but it just depended. You kind of hoped they'd be out. Now they have a scheme which I think is much better. They have a tremendous gathering in the officers' club, and they have little tables all over the place. For instance, if you were a golfer, somebody sits at the golf table. And supposing you were crazy about sailing, suppose you're crazy about singing and wanted to belong to the singing group. I forget what they call it at the moment. Supposing you belonged to any special thing like that, painting, or what have you.

Also, the Preservation Society has a table and the DAR has a table, and any interest that you specially have, you can go and find that table and talk to them and perhaps sign up.* And you know out of the huge mobs--I don't know how many there are, heaps, out of the whole push you don't have to just go around hunting. You know what I mean. You can call up Tom, Dick, and Harry, and say, "Look, let's have a golf game." So you have a chance to really get to know people. You have something to go on.

Q: Yes, a common interest.

Mrs. Smith: That was Kalbfus's idea that you can go and call on them and talk along and find out. They're newcomers, and you say, "What are your special interests? Are you interested in that? Do you want to belong to the art association?" You know. So it had its--and what's more he himself called on everybody and if you were out, he came again. This threw some of the young ones into fits. But still, it was probably good for them. And Mrs. Kalbfus, I think, hated this business because she would come to call and simply sit and not say a word. And I've seen her at cocktail parties...

Q: How lovely.

---
*DAR--Daughters of the American Revolution.

Mrs. Smith: Awful! She didn't do that to me because, after all, we've known each other when. Not that--I was a kid and she was grown up and married, you know, but still. He was very gregarious. He loved parties, loved to go places, and he used to say over and over and it was his theory, and I think he was right--he said, "The only way you were going to get to know your young officers is to go out and socialize with them, and you can't do it formally. The way to do it is to go out and be where they are and talk to them. Go to cocktail parties and come first and stay until the last ditch and sashay around and talk to everybody"--most friendly and chatting.

Q: And she was just like a dead weight?

Mrs. Smith: She'd sit in the front hall, sit on a sofa somewhere and just say nothing.

Q: Why didn't he excuse her from going at all?

Mrs. Smith: That was his problem, not mine. But I can see her now sitting in a not very large house, you know, and she'd sit in the living room on a sofa near the door or something like that, and the poor hostess would be going out of her mind. Here's the senior lady sitting off here, and you've got to attend to the senior lady's pleasure and comfort, and you've also got to attend to your guests. She didn't like parties like that.

Q: She certainly realized what problems she created for the hostess.

Mrs. Smith: I don't think she cared. I don't know. I don't know. She used to go off on long trips. After he died, she went on that trip to Africa by herself and somebody asked her if she minded going by herself, and she said no, she didn't mind at all. She was taken ill on that trip and died, and was taken somewhere in Africa to a hospital. I don't know what happened to her. But anyway, she didn't have any children. I don't know what she would do. But we were very festive then. There were lots of parties, lots of goings on. This is when we had the Torpedo Station party and the Fort Adams party and the War College party, and they were real parties, I'm telling you. They had boxes around. Where did we go? I suppose it's the family theater now. Boxes around there all like that, and Bellevue Avenue came. Bellevue Avenue in those days used to call up and invite, say, "I would like three or four young men to come."

Q: Unattached young men.

Mrs. Smith: Unattached young men. Because way past that, after my younger daughter's husband was killed in the war and she was with me, this young--there were three unattached British officers there, and a friend of mine's husband had been on duty in Charleston when the British ships came in for repairs and that kind of thing, so she had known a couple of them. She telephoned and said--my daughter being a widow, she was very pretty and, of course, young, and she said, "I have no wish to be married again, and I'm tired of being shown all these people." She said, "All these unattached men at the right age, either nobody understands them or they're so stuck on themselves they're not fit, and I'm through with them." So anyhow, we dragged her to the party--not the party, but she went over finally, and first thing I knew, here she is engaged to Horace, our young British officer.* And he was trying hard to date her, and he was interminably having to go down to Mrs. Vanderbilt's and have dinner. It killed him, because the senior office in charge of those three, Captain Hawkins, took very seriously the social angle on Bellevue Avenue. And when word came that bachelors were needed, these three, of course, were right in there, no escape. They couldn't say, "This is my night out," or anything.

Q: Command performance.

Mrs. Smith: It was command performance, that's right. So many, many times, he'd find himself sent down to Bellevue Avenue to sit and dine on a gold plate with a footman behind him, and conversation didn't particularly amuse him, but playing his part in it, feed him to the teeth, I'm telling you. He still thinks about it.

---
*Commander Horace George Barnard, RN.

Q: Maybe that was one of his incentives for hurrying up and getting married so he could be excused.

Mrs. Smith: No, he didn't get married then. The British Government, I thought, was very smart. They said when they finished that course at the college, then they must not come straight home; they must see something of the United States. They were required to go--I think it was three things, see a big industrial plant or a steel mill, or I don't know what.

Q: What you might call a cook's tour they had to take.

Mrs. Smith: Yes, except they could choose it, because these three bought an ancient wreck of a car and they drove down South, way South, and then across the country. Horace wanted to go fishing in the Black Hills of South Dakota, and one of them wanted to go to Yosemite, and one of them wanted to do something in the South, I've forgotten what. So they went way South, then they went across and then they went up, and then they came back over. So they had quite a feast of the United States by the time they got back. When they got back, then came the wedding, and they took off for England. And Horace is very--I said to him, "Well, thank goodness, you're Navy, because if you weren't, I wouldn't talk to you at all."

Q: Did he continue to make a career of the Royal Navy?

Mrs. Smith: Well, he stayed in the Royal Navy. As a matter of fact, he was in the Battle of River Plate, in the Exeter, when little ships chased the big ship. And he was . . .

Q: The Graf Spee.

Mrs. Smith: Yes. When he was at the College, when they were engaged, a friend of my husband's asked me if I would like him—my husband had died, you see—if I would like him to look up his record.* After all, I didn't know anything about him, here he is, just a young man from England. And he did, and he came back and had a marvelous record, all this stuff, which was fine. But it's rather going off into the blue, you might say.

Q: Has he retired now?

Mrs. Smith: I was going to say, then he went abroad, of course, went back home and served in various ships, and he served in the Vanguard, and there was a tremendous exercise at sea.** Roy was there in something else from here. And they had a tremendous storm, and the Vanguard cracked right across; a crack appeared across her main deck, and she was hurried into dry dock. This was supposed to be kept a big secret, nothing said. And then the

---
*Commander Roy C. Smith, USN (Ret.) died at the Newport Naval Hospital on 1 June 1946.
**HMS Vanguard was the last battleship built for the Royal Navy; she was completed in 1946.

admiral couldn't make up his mind whether he wished to repair her or scrap her or what. And Horace was the exec. It was a very good job. He was young for the job he had. After War College, he was the youngest commander in the British Navy. So he was doing fine. And then the captain got wind of what was going to happen. The ship was going to stay in dry dock, so he beat it up to the Admiralty and got himself transferred. And as soon as Horace got the idea--he didn't have any friends in senior people in the admiralty, I guess, he tried to get off, too, and they said, "No, no, no, you cannot do that. You are the exec and you must stay." So he stayed in command of the thing in dry dock. And while there, he came up for selection. They told him, apparently, or they told Lou that he was still very young on the list and the admiralty felt it was only fair to give some of the older ones who wouldn't have another chance, a chance, and he'd have another chance, and besides, he was still in the dry dock. So that he was not selected, which was a severe blow, as you can imagine. But you could see how it would be. And with his record, there's no reason to suppose he wouldn't have been selected, really. I mean, you can say he might and he might not. But still, with his record as it was. So just about then, of course, he had been married, and just about then--you know, after that, they threw their Navy away, the way we do.

Q: Oh, yes.

Mrs. Smith: There was the Navy paid and the Navy free, having to do with tobacco. Apparently that's what it meant, and I don't know, tax or something. But anyhow, the Navy then looked just like when Roy got out. He could stay in in the reserve and he could go down to a place in the South and sit on reserve ships, you know. And Horace felt that his future was strictly clouded, and he was offered a job, a very good job with Vickers for as much pay, and he felt, after all, he had been married before, unhappily. His wife had gone off with somebody else and left him while he was at sea, which rather embittered him about females. He had no more idea of getting married than Lou did. They both were agin the idea. However, it didn't do him any good, so in all events, he did retire and took the job with Vickers and was with them quite a long time, quite a long time. They eventually went to Mexico and he's now--I don't know what they did, but anyway, he's not with them anymore. They live in Southampton, and he's with a firm that does something I should think would be rather interesting. I don't know if there are many people in the firm. They take a ship coming in. Of course, there's nothing coming in now but oilers and tankers, I gather. We don't seem to have anything else. But anyway, a ship coming in will wire ahead and say they've got a boiler damaged or engine trouble or something, and he is supposed, then, to find the proper person and the proper--whatever they need, and have it ready on the dock, so when the ship comes in, people can rush on, fix it, and it saves thousands of dollars in wharfage or dockage, whatever the word is, you know. So that ship can go right on its way instead of being delayed. He has to telephone sometimes or get in touch with ships all over the world, because all kinds of ships come in, you know, and have it air-mailed, or whatever it is. But I should think that would be rather interesting, and I should think it would go forward, I don't know. But he's now reached the great age of 62 or 63 or something, so I suppose he's--you know how that is. I don't know what they do over there.

Q: About retirement?

Mrs. Smith: I don't know what they do, either.

Q: Well, let's get back. You were going from Newport after your tour of duty there to Panama.

Mrs. Smith: Yes. We went to Panama.

Q: Tell me about Panama.

Mrs. Smith: Well, Panama in those days was quite surprising.

Q: This was what date?

Mrs. Smith: Well, this must have been--let's see. We came back to the War College in the winter of '32. So we must have been in Panama in '30-'31, just about there. We got down there and, of course, we were no use at all. I mean to say we had no rank. The gentleman running everything was Army, you know, what do you call him?

Q: He was a general and he was in command of the base.

Mrs. Smith: That's right. He was. And then, of course, when it comes to houses, Army, all the way down to the bottom, the Special Service Squadron began with admiral and all down at the bottom, and when it got down to us, it was nothing.

Q: Your husband was what rank then?

Mrs. Smith: He was then ...

Q: Commander?

Mrs. Smith: He was commander, that's right. He was the navigator in the USS *Memphis*.

Q: He didn't have sufficient rank to get quarters?

Mrs. Smith: Nobody had any quarters. Don't be silly. Quarters--there were no such thing. Maybe the Army got quarters, but us Navy didn't, I tell you. We were Special Service Squadron. We were trash. So anyhow, he got down there ahead before me, because I was staying in Annapolis and finishing up the girls' school. And we got down there, finally, and he had found--in those days, you could rent the houses of zone people, and they would go on leave, you see. They were entitled to so much leave a year.

Q: In the canal zone.

Mrs. Smith: The canal zone, that's right. And then they had leave without pay, so they quit going on leave. They stayed. And we moved five times in that year, so you can imagine, I was right busy.

Q: Bouncing around from one house to another.

Mrs. Smith: From one house to the next, that's right, and we finally moved out near the Miramont Club out in Panama, you might say. It was hopeless; there wasn't anything else. And it seemed to me I spent my whole time dashing to and fro, because the speed limit was five miles an hour. And I had to take him to work and the girls to school, him to the ship, the girls to school, and I had to get the girls.

Q: What kind of a car were you driving?

Mrs. Smith: We took down our Buick with us. But my younger daughter was very blonde and extravagantly pretty, if I do say so, she really was.* They were both pretty but she was very blonde, she had very lovely golden-yellow hair, you know, and in that country, you stood out like a sore thumb. Walking down the street, we'd have people walking along behind us looking at her, you know. It was awful. But anyway, I used to pick her up and take her to school. I had an awful time with a policeman, because he'd lie and wait for me, and if I went six miles an hour, he'd stop me and he'd get out his book and he'd be sitting there looking at Lou like this, "Ah!" just gazing at her. "She's more beautiful than the stars," says he. Talking with his book. I could have killed him. Every two minutes I was stopped, and nothing happens except I'm stopped and he gazes.

Q: He didn't give you a ticket or anything?

Mrs. Smith: No, he didn't give me a ticket. He only stopped me to look at Lou, you see. My other daughter, by this time, had come back home. I had a time with him, and if you don't think it took half my day to and from at five miles an hour . . .

Q: What did it do to your daughter?

---

*The younger Smith daughter is Louisa Taylor Smith, born 27 April 1917.

Mrs. Smith: Well, fortunately, she had a very good sense of humor and still has, and she's always been, from the time she was very, very small, people have always stopped her and said how beautiful she was, pretty she was. Now, of course, she's older and she's got more wrinkles, so to speak, but she was extravagantly pretty. And that's always been part of her life, and it never went to her head. I don't think she ever paid any attention, really. I mean, if you were born without a hand, I suppose, you'd get used to it. People would stop. People don't stop commenting on that. I used to say, "Heavens, it doesn't matter. That dress is all right. Nobody's going to look."

She'd say, "Yes, they do." And I'd go out with her, and they would. They did. They gazed upon her in all directions.

But otherwise, Panama--we didn't do anything much except move and that kind of thing.

Q: Wasn't that hard on the children in school?

Mrs. Smith: Yes, very, very. Yes, it was very hard on them. The result was they never got educated. We always thought we would have all four of our children educated and graduate from college and able to support themselves and look out for themselves. Roy got bounced from the Academy, from there he goes out to Michigan, he does graduate from Michigan, he starts--this is demerits, you know what I mean, because he, as a midshipman, he just did silly things. Nothing was really bad. I mean, for instance, they all went out one night--he played on the water polo team, and they all went out one hot night and swam in the pool. Forbidden. And the watchman--I'd known the watchman because we had duty there and lived on King George Street when Roy was small, and the watchmen were the the same old ones. They said to me, "Mrs. Smith, it's too bad because we know your boy and the others, the whole crowd of them, they run off and we don't know any of them, so your boy gets on the pap." So Roy got himself a tremendous reputation for being indifferent to rules, and it caught up with him, just terrible. It almost killed him. It certainly was an awful blow to us, too. I've lost where I was.

Q: Well, you were in Panama, and I'd asked you if it wasn't difficult for the children.

Mrs. Smith: Well, yes. Roy was at the Academy then and being naughty, you know, and the girls were going to school and dating all over the place. Bobby Molten was in command, who was an old-time beau of mine to some extent, was in command of the air base at Coco Solo.* We went out on a ship with him and the girls were 15 and 17. I couldn't lock Lou up; I couldn't afford to leave her behind in boarding school. And she was conspicuous, shall I say.

---
*Commander Robert P. Molten, Jr., USN.

Q: How old was she at that point?

Mrs. Smith: Fifteen, going on 16. Lou was 16. Mary was two years older. And Bobby said to me, "I want her to come over and stay with us at Coco Solo. I'll give her a good time with all the young aviators."

I said, "She's too young."

He said, "Well, I'll look out for her. I'll take good care of her." But what are you going to do with her? Put her in a closet? Can't put a curtain over her head, can you? Know what I mean? And she was much too young to be running around with those people, but it didn't worry them any. It certainly didn't worry her any. No, she had a very good, cheerful time. But anyway, they were going to school. They were going to high school. They weren't doing so hot. And the climate didn't agree with Mary, so she came home, and my youngest son was there going to school, and just going around like kids do, you know. There wasn't very much to do, but still.

Then we were ordered home, and there was still ...

Q: Then in a sense you were glad to be ordered home, weren't you?

Mrs. Smith: I was just as glad to leave Panama, yes, because I had nervous fits about the girls. I found out afterwards, you see, that Lou had done this little rash thing. Her sister had gone home. I don't know if it made any difference or not. And so then we were ordered home, and you have to go when you are ordered because it was leave without pay stuff. If you didn't go when you were ordered, you could stay there 'til goodness knows when the government would get around to you. So I went to the head of the--it was just before, well, about three weeks before the final exams. I went to the principal and said, "Look, we have to go home. Can't you give Lou and Monty exams early so they'll have some credits when they get home?"

And he said, "Certainly not." He said, "We're sick and tired of these Navy children or service children asking for special things. Certainly not. No, no, no. Can't do anything about it."

So we came home. They had no credits at all. The year they'd spent in Panama didn't count. So then we sent Monty to boarding school.

Q: Did they do anything about the language while they were there? Did they acquire the Spanish language?

Mrs. Smith: No, nobody spoke Spanish. I mean, nobody that we knew spoke Spanish, and we didn't know any Spanish people. There were some Navy people who had a large circle of Spanish friends, but we didn't know any of them. In fact, we didn't know very many people.

Q: I suppose you couldn't because you were moving so much.

Mrs. Smith: Yes, we were. And then various ships came in. A German ship came in and had to be entertained, and a British ship came in and had to be entertained, a Japanese ship came in, and I don't remember if it was entertained. The Japanese ship was funny because along the dock, they docked Memphis and others like this, you know, in row, and the Japanese ship immediately had a little sort of sentry box down by the gangway. Nobody else did. It was all very secret, you know, and they had some curtain over the side of the ship up here so you couldn't see anything. I don't know what you'd want to see. But that sort of thing went on. I don't remember we did anything. My life was too agitated, you might say. Oh, then my husband developed a bad sinus, so that wasn't so hot. And the ship took off. We went on the ship through the canal over to Coco Solo and visited there. Of course, the ship coming down stopped at Coco Solo, and then we went on to Panama. No, I was glad that year was up.

Then we got home. We went back to Newport, and of course, the girls had no standing at all as far as school went; neither did Monty. We tried to put Monty in St. George's School, which is good, and they wouldn't have him, they said unless he fitted in perfectly. We said we'd have him tutored. They said, "No, no, no. He's got to fit." So then he went to Severn. Monty went to boarding school, and the girls struggled along in high school and never did much with it. Mary never graduated it, neither did Lou. So they never got educated. And somebody said to me the other day, one of my grandsons, Roy IV's classmates is now--when he was a midshipman, my mother was living on Southgate Avenue and he used to bring out, same as my brother did, who was in '16, bring out four or five or six or eight boys to lunch and dinner every Saturday and Sunday. And one of these chaps, Sweetser, is now a lieutenant colonel; he's now married and has three children.* And my grandson is 6'6" and he was just that tall, even taller, and they called me up the other day. They're now on duty in Newport. He's going to the War College. It gave me quite a turn. I hadn't seen him since he was 18 or 19. I used to come down and stay with my mother, you see, at intervals, and all these boys would come pouring out, and I knew Skip then. And here I knew him at 19, and now I see him with three children and a wife, very much grown up, a big change all around. Well, I don't know.

Coming back from Panama was, as I said, well, that first year we had was all those things happened. Then after that, things sort of settled down.

Q: At the War College, you mean?

Mrs. Smith: At the War College. Then we left there and went to Honolulu.

Q: What was your husband's job at the War College?

---
*Lieutenant Colonel Warren E. Sweetser III, USMC.

Mrs. Smith: He was on the staff. First he was a student and then he was on the staff.

Q: Did he teach, or just the administrative staff?

Mrs. Smith: No, no. He taught. He was in--oh, dear, what was it? What do you call it when you have war games?

Q: War games, I guess they call it.

Mrs. Smith: They used to have war games. You ought to see what they've got now. That's real electronic junk.

Q: I understand, yes. I haven't seen it, but I understand.

Mrs. Smith: Well, they used to have war games. He was in tactics, they call it. I don't know what the name of it was. And then after he retired, we went back there after Honolulu, where he was taken ill. We came back and we based in Newport eventually, and he used to go to the college and have a lot of fun, because he had a friend, Jerry Tiernan, who was retired because he got something wrong with his throat.* And they used to go together and the college gave them a room and a typewriter, and my husband's father was a naval attache in Paris when he was growing up, so he spoke French just like English. So he did a

---
*Lieutenant Thomas Jerome Tiernan, USN.

lot of translating. They had a lot of Clausewitz and things like that.* He translated at sight, and Jerry would type. They had a lovely time, you know. They thoroughly enjoyed this.

Q: Yes, yes.

Mrs. Smith: And meanwhile, Mary got married, Roy got married, and they all grew up.

Q: But this was after you were retired.

Mrs. Smith: Yes, after we retired, yes.

Q: Continue on with the career. He was on the staff at the Naval War College.

Mrs. Smith: He was on the staff at the War College, that's right; he was there three years. Then when he was here on duty, he was assistant editor of the Naval Institute while he was teaching engineering.

Q: When was this?

Mrs. Smith: This is when we were here on duty at first. Well, this was . . .

---
*Major General Karl von Clausewitz, Prussian army officer best remembered for his books on the science of war.

Q: This was before you went to China.

Mrs. Smith: Before we went to China.

Q: Yes, you did talk about that.

Mrs. Smith: Then after that, then, of course, everything was cut short from Honolulu.

Q: Tell me about going to Honolulu.

Mrs. Smith: Honolulu was really great fun. He had command of the Oglala, which he thoroughly enjoyed, except it burned him to a crisp because Admiral Neal was the admiral, and Neal didn't want to go anywhere.* My husband was convinced that it would be very important to map all of the area out there, which never did get done until the war came.

Q: You mean the islands?

Mrs. Smith: Not only the Hawaiian islands, no, but the whole area.

Q: The whole Pacific area.

---

*Rear Admiral George F. Neal, USN, Commander Minecraft Battle Force.

Mrs. Smith: The whole Pacific area, yes, as far as you could go.

Q: What time period was this, when you went out there?

Mrs. Smith: Well, let's see. When we went out there, it must have been '31, '30.

Q: It must have been after that.

Mrs. Smith: Well, '33? I don't remember. No, Roy got himself bounced out of the Academy while we were on duty at the War College--Roy would have graduated in '34. So we must have gone to Honolulu in the spring of '35, and we were out there for a year before he became ill. But he loved having the ship, naturally, but he was always trying to go out, and the Oglala was a mine layer.

Q: Yes, I know she was, yes. But she was equipped for hydrographic work?

Mrs. Smith: She was, and he thought it was dreadful. They should go out and do it. He thought it was terribly important, that the government did not have proper maps for the whole area. He would have gone all over the lot. I don't know where he wouldn't have gone.

Q: Why did the admiral object to that?

Mrs. Smith: Because he didn't like going to sea.

Q: But by that time, of course, it was in the future, but some of the more farseeing naval officers who anticipated an eventual war with Japan...

Mrs. Smith: Anyway, well, they weren't very farseeing. Look what happened. And when we were there, I mean, driving down to Pearl, to the ship, on Dillingham Boulevard, at the gate were great big oil tanks sitting there--nearby at least, you know, and my husband used to have a fit. He said this would be the easiest place in the world to bomb, it would be terrible trouble if you could, and Admiral Richardson came out while we were there, and he had screaming fits.* He said, "This is terrible. This is awful." We saw him at a party. Well, I'm not saying he talked as free as that, but I mean, that was the idea. He said, "Here is the fleet all bottled up like this here." And he was going back to complain bitterly about it to the President, and he did go back, and he got transferred to another job. And we had Pearl Harbor as a result, I mean, in the end. But the ships were bunched there, you know, and the air base was there; everything was there, all handy, convenient. And I tell you, my husband--

---

*Admiral James O. Richardson, USN, Commander in Chief U.S. Fleet from January 1940 to February 1941.

well, he was a student of history, anyway, and he said he thought it was terrible. They ought to really be doing some serious hydrographic work. And every time they'd go to sea, he'd say to me, "Now I'm going to sea Monday morning and we'll probably be back Friday or Saturday." They'd come back Wednesday. And George Neal--I don't know what he had, something wrong with his foot, cellulitis or something fancy like that. He'd have to come back and check with the doctor. But anyhow, they came back, they came in, they kept coming in, because Pa would come home boiling with rage because he wanted to go out. It was fine with me having him come back, but just the same, he said, "This is dreadful. We're not doing at all what we ought to be doing." He didn't get anywhere.

Q: There was a group of sister ships to the Oglala, were there not?

Mrs. Smith: No.

Q: Weren't there other minesweepers there?

Mrs. Smith: Not that I remember.

Q: I thought there were two or three.

Mrs. Smith: There may have been. I don't remember them.

Q: The admiral was in command of what?

Mrs. Smith: He lived aboard the Oglala.

Q: That was his flagship.

Mrs. Smith: That was his flagship.

Q: But what other ships did he have in his ...

Mrs. Smith: I don't really remember, to tell you the truth. I should but I don't. I just remember him, because I used to go down and play mah-jongg on board all the time, and give my husband thousands of fits because George and Molly and his wife and another gal and I used to go down. George encouraged, asked us to sit in his cabin and play mah-jongg all day long. My husband said, "This is dreadful, this is dreadful. I wish you wouldn't."

I said, "Listen, you better have me, because if it isn't me, it's going to be some other gal. It might as well be me. I'll do my best to be quiet." But it's true. He would come in as the captain, and George would get up maybe for a few minutes and come back, but he was a funny chap, George, pleasant, nice, I enjoyed playing games with him but my husband did not enjoy having it go on like that.

Q: George Dyer was out there at the same time, wasn't he?*

Mrs. Smith: I don't know. I didn't know him.

Q: You knew him in Annapolis?

Mrs. Smith: No.

Q: Vice Admiral George Dyer?

Mrs. Smith: No. Don't know him. Most of the vice admirals were too young for me to know.

Q: George isn't.

Mrs. Smith: Baby children.

Q: George isn't. He's pushing 80.

Mrs. Smith: Well, I might know him but I don't remember him. Then, you see, we were there, we went out in the spring, I guess it was, yes. We finished here and went out there, and then we hadn't been there just about a year when he had this business.

---

*Vice Admiral George C. Dyer, USN, whose reminiscences are contained in the Naval Institute's oral history collection. As a commander in the late 1930s, he served on Admiral Richardson's U.S. Fleet staff.

His ankle swelled up and I said, "You'd better go and talk to the doctor about it." He made a fuss, but finally he did, and the doctor put him in the hospital and operated, and then told me that he didn't know if anything was the matter much, and they'd send a slice of this thing to Bethesda. And Queens Hospital checked and their hospital checked, and they didn't think it was anything, so on and so on. So then they're having war games, and right in the middle of radio silence comes the word to break radio silence and send him home at once. So we had three days to get organized and leave. So we lived at the Nimau Hotel, which was very pleasant, little cottages all scattered around. We knew some people that were in town. We had the Scotts, who were old friends, and Scott himself was a friend of King Kalakaua's, whatever his name was, and he grew up on the islands. We used to go out and walk. Not walk, but you know. And he married this gal whom my husband had known in New York, so we saw them and their friends, but they were strictly civilian. They weren't Navy. The Whitings were there, and the Whiting girl was a great friend of my Mary's.

Q: Which Whiting was this?

Mrs. Smith: The aviator. Kenneth, I think.

Q: Kenneth Whiting, yes.*

---

*Captain Kenneth Whiting, USN, Naval Aviator #16.

Mrs. Smith: That's right. Because then we got ordered home in three days. Meanwhile, my Mary had met Peter Staley, whose ship had come in and gone out in the Navy way, and she said, "I'd like to stay in the hotel and follow you home."*

We said, "You can't do that."

And she said, "Well, I have to wait and see Peter again. I don't know if I really mean it or he means it or what." And she said, "Well, can I stay if I stay with the Whitings?"

And I said, "Well, I don't know Mrs. Whiting from a hole in the wall." I'd say how-do-you-do at a party, yes.

So Mrs. Whiting called me up with a rather chilly voice and said she'd be glad to have Mary stay. I knew darned well she wouldn't, but it was Mary's life, the heck with Mrs. Whiting.

So we rushed home to the hospital, and Memorial, all that mess. And they stayed.

Q: Apparently it was a malignancy?

Mrs. Smith: Well, they said it was filicula lymphycarocoma, which is cancer of the lymph glands. And in those days—now they can do something about it, but then they didn't know anything to do about it at all. They told me he probably would live just a few months, maybe. They told him he was going to get fine and go back to duty. They told me, "Remain cheerful and gay, don't tell your children, say nothing to nobody. Just remain normal."

―――――――――――
*Lieutenant (junior grade) Poyntell C. Staley, Jr., USN.

So he said to me, "Why do you mind so much my being not selected?" Well, I couldn't say, "Because I'm afraid you're dying." So I put on as bold a show as I could.

People used to say to me, "It's lucky it's you and not me, because I would not be able to do it." It's surprising what you can do if you have to. It's surprising. That's why these people that fall down and can't get up all surprise me. I bet you could crawl to the phone if you had to. Maybe that'll be my fate and I won't crawl to the phone, I don't know.

But we were only in Honolulu for about a year, just about a year, and it was lovely. It really was lovely.

Q: It came to a very quick and sad end.

Mrs. Smith: It came to a quick and sad end, that's right.

Q: Did your daughter marry this chap?

Mrs. Smith: Peter? Yes. He's now a retired naval aviator. Both my girls married aviators. I said, "What do you think you're doing? Trying to scare me to death?" One came through, and one was killed.

Q: Do you know the Whiting daughter?

Mrs. Smith: Eddie? She's Mrs. Nisewaner now.

Q: Yes, and lives in Bethesda.

Mrs. Smith: Yes, I know Eddie. Sure. I knew her out here and I've known her since. They had duty in Newport one time. Yes, I like Eddie. My Mary was down there staying with her. She was there again with her. No, Eddie's great, and he's nice, too. His name I forget at the moment.

Q: I don't know him.

Mrs. Smith: Well, that's something. He came to see me a while ago, which was nice of him. Well, I don't know. Our career was cut short, and that's one reason why I feel when Mrs. Eccles says to me, "Coffee ranks tea," in other words, "Henry ranks your husband."* So he does. He's alive. I don't mean to say I cared. It just amused me, rather. It's like in my day, many an admiral's wife I've seen who's stalked ahead, you know, and sat in the best seat. Well, that's her right. You're getting into a steam launch with her and she gets in and plunks down, that's her right, she should. But some of them do it, you know, sort of, "Who are you, worm?" Especially when you're very junior.

Q: Sounds like a page from a long time past.

---

*Rear Admiral Henry E. Eccles, USN (Ret.), who lived in Newport at the time of the interview.

Mrs. Smith: It was a long time past. It was a long time past, it really was. It really was. I remember I was staying with my friend, who I'm going to see now, Margaret Parker, in Norfolk. Her father was captain of the yard at Portsmouth. And Cousin Billy Rodgers was then Captain Rodgers, in command of the Georgia.* And he asked us out for dinner, and we accepted, naturally, with pleasure, and we thought he might ask--she had a beau on one ship, and my fiance was in South Carolina, and Cousin Billy said, "Of course, I'm not going to have any of those people. You're going to go out with my people from the Georgia." So we go to Georgia, didn't have a very good time, and I nearly died of fright because naturally I sat on his right and the stewards in those days had the most beautiful, fancy foods. And they cut vegetables in the shape of roses and flowers and stuff, you know, you've seen that. And made mashed potatoes like green waves, you know.

Q: Yes, the way the Japanese do things.

Mrs. Smith: Well, this was a Japanese steward he had. Yes. So they bring it on, and here I am, they bring in a fish about this long, and the fish--I don't know if it was done in gelatin, but it was all shiny, you know, glittery, his tail turned up like that, and its eyes were there and the whole thing was all

---

*Captain William L. Rodgers, USN, commanding officer of the USS Georgia (BB-15) from 1910 to 1911.

perfect, and they had the sea of green mashed potatoes all around, you know. I thought, "How do I attack this? How in the name of heaven do you attack this?" I didn't want to take a knife and make a sort of messy hole in the middle of this beautiful object. I didn't know what to do with it. I said, "No, thank you."

And Cousin Billy said, "Don't be a fool, Mary. Have some," which embarrassed me, being 18, before the whole company, you know what I mean. So I scratch a hole in the thing, dying of terror--well, not terror, but embarrassment, you might say. But in those days they had very fancy foods for a ship and, of course, they had a wine mess aboard ship. I went out to Old Point to pursue the South Carolina, and that was the time they reenacted the battle of something or other down there. And they had the Army in, you know; they had all kinds of stuff. My husband was in charge of transportation from the ships in. He hated it. He had to live in a tent, and he found it very disagreeable, indeed. It was all very exciting, you know, bringing millions of people in. But it's a checkered career, as you might say.

Q: An interesting one, nevertheless.

Mrs. Smith: Well, it is, yes.

Q: It takes you to all corners of the world.

Mrs. Smith: Well, yes, it really is, and I loved going to Gibraltar. Roy had duty there, and it was fascinating. I loved Gibraltar. Of course, Lou married to an Englishman, I've been there several times. My husband's friend, Admiral England, who was up at Nanking when that fracas came off, lives in Ireland, and so I went over to see Lou and Horace, and I went to see him, and he met me in Dublin, and we went all around the place.* He had staying with him also Mrs. Macartney, whose husband was in the Standard Oil business when ships were upriver, up the Nanking. And she was there and we had a great ten days.

Q: You had some common background.

Mrs. Smith: Yes, but I had never seen her before and I'd never been upriver before. I didn't dare. I couldn't go upriver.

Q: But still, it was the ...

Mrs. Smith: That's right. It was fun, and Hugh was great fun, too. He's still going, apparently. I have a Christmas card from him every year. But I don't know what he's like now, because he must be 90 something. I guess he's 92 or 91 or something like that.

---

*Admiral Hugh T. England, RN. In March 1927 as a captain in command of HMS Emerald, England worked with Mrs. Smith's husband to establish an evacuation plan for American and British missionaries and businessmen trapped in Nanking when the Chinese Southern Army attacked the city.

Index to

Series of Taped Interviews

with

Mrs. Marc A. Mitscher

and

Mrs. Roy C. Smith, Jr.

Akron, USS (ZRS-4)
   Mitscher's friend Commander Cecil killed in April 1933 crash, p. 13; quirk of fate keeps Mitscher from fatal flight, pp. 31-32

Alger, Captain Philip R., USN (USNA, 1880)
   As professor of mathematics at the Naval Academy in the early 1900s, pp. 64-65; drinking habits, p. 68; secretary-treasurer of the U.S. Naval Institute in the early 1900s, pp. 83-84, 110, 113-115, 191; physical fitness buff, p. 84; love of music, p. 98; predicts future of submarines in early 1900s, pp. 107-108; death in February 1912, p. 110

Annapolis, Maryland
   Proximity of private homes to the Naval Academy, pp. 70-71; public schools in the early 1900s, pp. 75-76; description of town in early 1900s, pp. 76-77, 80; social activities in the early 1900s, pp. 98, 103, 115

Aviation
   See Naval Aviation

Barnard, Commander Horace G., RN
   Meets and marries Louise Smith Stevens at Newport in the late 1940s, pp. 197-199; service in HMS Exeter during World War II, p. 200; service in HMS Vanguard in the 1950s, pp. 200-201; civilian employment, pp. 202-203

Barnard, Louise Smith
   To her brother's chagrin, dates his company commander in the early 1930s, pp. 88-89; breaks arm as child in Shanghai in the mid-1920s, pp. 170-173; meets third husband in Newport after World War II, pp. 197-199; appearance causes stir in Panama in the early 1930s, pp. 206-209; education, pp. 210-211

Boxer Rebellion
   Mrs. Smith's recollections of her family's participation in 1900, p. 109

Burke, Admiral Arleigh A., USN (USNA, 1923)
   Mrs. Mitscher's friendship with Admiral Burke, pp. 26-27

Charleston Navy Yard
   Description of hospital in the early 1920s, p. 134

Chaumont, USS (AP-5)
   Takes congressmen to China on junket in 1925, pp. 138-139

China
    USS Noa (DD-343) sent to Nanking in 1927, p. 94; Congressmen take junket to China in 1925, pp. 138-139, 155-156; customs regulations in the mid-1920s, p. 141; accommodations, pp. 140, 142-147, 150-151, 154; description of Shanghai in the mid-1920s, pp. 142-143, 145-149; currency, pp. 149, 153-154, 158; social activities, p. 155; Smith children attend American-run schools, pp. 154-157, 178-179; political situation in 1920s, pp. 139, 156, 176; mixed court, pp. 160-161; attitude towards Americans in the mid-1920s, pp. 156, 159-162, 177; quality of life, pp. 163-164, 168; medical services, pp. 164-166, 170-174; death and burial practices, pp. 166-168; missionaries, pp. 169-170, 177

Communications
    In Annapolis in the early 1900s, pp. 111-113

Congressional Junkets
    Congressmen visit China in the mid-1920s, pp. 138-139, 156

Conroy, James W.
    U.S. Naval Institute staff member offers assistance to Mrs. Alger after her husband's death in 1912, p. 114

England, Admiral Hugh T., RN
    Mrs. Smith keeps in touch with Royal Navy officer who worked with Lieutenant Commander Smith in 1927 to evacuate civilians in Nanking, p. 227

Food
    Liquor served with dinners during Prohibition, pp. 68, 91, 181; formal dinner parties in Newport in the late 1920s, pp. 90-91, 96-97, 182, 184-187; formal dinner parties at the Naval Academy in the early 1900s, pp. 91-93, 97-98; meals in China in the mid-1920s, p. 146; elaborate dinner in the battleship Georgia (BB-15) in the early 1910s, pp. 225-226

Georgia, USS (BB-15)
    Mary Alger uncomfortable at formal dinner in Georgia as guest of her cousin, the commanding officer, in the early 1910s, pp. 225-226

Hart, Admiral Thomas C., USN (USNA, 1897)
    Embarrassing trip during marching practice as drill instructor at the Naval Academy in the early 1900s, pp. 74-75, 101; dinner party etiquette, pp. 92-93; characterized as stiff and formal, p. 101; attitude towards Navy children and discipline, pp. 102, 181-182; son Roswell's academic troubles in the late 1920s, pp. 177-178, 182

Holland, USS (SS-1)
   At the Naval Academy in the early 1900s, pp. 107-108

Japan
   Admiral Mitscher's attitude toward Japanese, pp. 60-61; secrecy of Japanese ship visit to Panama in the early 1930s, p. 211

John Rodgers, USS (DD-983)
   Mrs. Smith sponsored ship named for her relatives at christening in March 1978, p. 118

Kalbfus, Rear Admiral Edward C., USN (USNA, 1899)
   Mrs. Smith's recollections of his courting of Captain Stimson Brown's daughter at the Naval Academy in the late 1890s, p. 191; increases social obligations at the Naval War College in the late 1930s, pp. 189, 191, 195-196; contrasts to his wife's social behavior, pp. 195-197

Kane, Captain John D., USN (USNA, 1918)
   Died while commanding officer in the USS New Orleans (CA-32) on 13 June 1944, p. 116

Liquor
   Use in Naval Academy entertaining in the early 1900s, pp. 68, 90-91; at Newport during Prohibition, pp. 179-182

Luckenbach, MV
   Escort duty during World War I, p. 123

McVay, Rear Admiral Charles B., Jr., USN (USNA, 1890)
   As Commander Yangtze Patrol in the mid-1920s, turns down Lieutenant Commander Smith's request to delay reporting to the Rizal to get his family settled, p. 140

Memphis, USS (CL-13)
   In Panama in the early 1930s, p. 211

Midway, Battle of
   Loss of Torpedo Squadron Eight in this June 1942 action, pp. 58-59

Military Benefits and Privileges
   Lack of Navy support for family moves in the 1910s and 1920s, pp. 94, 121-123, 132, 141; housing for duty in Panama in the 1930s, pp. 204-205; ranking among officers' wives, p. 224

Mitscher, Frances Smalley
    Meets husband and marries in January 1913, pp. 5-7, 43, 46-47; parents, pp. 7, 43, 46; miscarriage in May 1918 precludes children, p. 16; reunion with husband after transatlantic attempt in 1919, pp. 29-31; correspondence with husband during war, pp. 34-35, 38-39, 48, 61-62; birth and early years, p. 43; health, pp. 16, 44-45; handled all household finances, pp. 54-55

Mitscher, Admiral Marc A., USN   (USNA, 1910)
    As Deputy Chief of Naval Operations (Air) in the mid-1940s, pp. 2-3; as a public speaker, pp. 2-3, 34, 38; health, pp. 3-4, 17; as Commander Eighth Fleet in 1946, pp. 3-4; duty in Colorado (ACR-7) in the early 1910s, pp. 5-6; gunboat duty in the early 1910s, p. 6-7; example of impetuousness, p. 7; parents, pp. 8, 18, 60; duty in North Carolina (ACR-12) in the mid-1910s, p. 8; characteristics assessed by wife, pp. 12-13, 16-18, 41-42, 48, 52-53, 62; flight training at Pensacola in the mid-1910s, pp. 9-12, 28; social activities, pp. 12, 23-24, 44, 49; sense of humor, pp. 13-14; close-mouthed, pp. 12, 17; as husband, pp. 14-15, 33, 46, 57, 59; at Rockaway, New York, air station in 1918, p. 16; at Miami NAS, p. 17; as sportsman, pp. 19, 22-23, 27; religion and attitude towards death, pp. 20-21; as midshipman in the late 1900s, pp. 23, 50; personal habits, p. 25; NC-1 transatlantic attempt in 1919, pp. 29-31; reaction to 1941 Pearl Harbor attack, pp. 32-33; correspondence with wife during war, pp. 34-35, 38-39, 48, 61-62; example of modesty, pp. 35-36; as commanding officer of Hornet (CV-8) in 1941-1942, pp. 32, 58-59; as Commander Task Force 58, p. 35; trademark baseball cap, pp. 40-41; attitude toward women, pp. 48-49; appearance, pp. 49-50, 54, 59-60; tattoo on arm, p. 32; chivalrous action on California train ride, pp. 54-54; portrayal in media, pp. 55-56, 60-61; supposed hatred of Japanese, pp. 60-61; dates Mary Alger as a midshipman, p. 106

Moffett, Rear Admiral William A., USN   (USNA, 1890)
    Chance decision to take another officer as his aide saves Mitscher from fatal flight in the Akron (ZRS-4) in April 1933, pp. 31-32

Molten, Commander Robert P., Jr., USN   (USNA, 1911)
    Friend of the Smiths offers to let Louise Smith live with his family at Coco Solo in the early 1930s, pp. 208-209

Mustin, Corinne (Mrs. Henry C. Mustin)
    Becomes Mrs. Mitscher's first service friend in 1915, pp. 10-11, 49

Naval Academy, U.S.
   Mitscher involved in hazing in the mid-1900s, pp. 50-51; Mitscher punished for drinking in room in 1907, but punishment dropped, pp. 51-52; professors at turn of century discussed, pp. 64-66; description of Academy grounds in the early 1900s, pp. 66-67, 69-73, 85, 95-96, 99-100, 190; Army-Navy football games in the early 1900s, pp. 67-68; security guards in the early 1900s, pp. 71-72; social activities in the early 1900s, pp. 78-79, 87; reputation of Annapolis girls, pp. 77-78; hops, pp. 83-89; sailing, pp. 89, 106; vessels assigned to the Academy in the early 1900s, pp. 106-108; graduates designated as passed midshipmen instead of ensigns for two years in the early 1900s, pp. 108, 110

Naval Aviation
   Antagonism from non-aviators, pp. 28-29; Mitscher's praise for World War II pilots in fast carrier task group, p. 35; both Smith girls marry World War II aviators, p. 223

Naval Institute, U.S.
   Mrs. Smith's recollections of her father's duty with the Naval Institute as secretary-treasurer in the early 1900s, pp. 113-115

Naval War College
   Social activities in the late 1920s, pp. 96-97, 101; social activities in the 1940s, pp. 192-198; Commander Smith translates for the Naval War College after retirement in 1937, pp. 213-214

NC Boats
   See Transatlantic Flight

Neal, Rear Admiral George F., USN (USNA, 1901)
   As Commander Minecraft Battle Force in the mid-1930s, doesn't share his flagship skipper Smith's interest in mapping Pacific area, pp. 215-218; assessed by Mrs. Smith, p. 219

Newport, Rhode Island
   Social activities in the 1920-1940s, pp. 96-97, 101, 178-189, 191-198; torpedo station in the late 1920s, pp. 177-178; Commander Smith translates for the Naval War College after retirement in 1937, pp. 213-214

Noa, USS (DD-343)
   Roy Smith III serves as a powder monkey at Nanking in 1927, pp. 94-95, 176; Lieutenant Commander Smith picked up by Rizal (DD-174) in Shanghai in 1925 to be taken to his new command, the Noa, p. 140; Smith takes command of Noa during a typhoon, pp. 151-152

Panama
   Housing accommodations in the early 1930s, pp. 204-205; Louise Smith creates stir, pp. 206-209; foreign ships visit in the early 1930s, pp. 210-211

Pearl Harbor, Hawaiian Islands
   Marc Mitscher's reaction to December 1941 attack, pp. 32-33; Commander Smith wanted to map Pacific area as commanding officer of the Oglala (CM-4) in the mid-1930s, pp. 215-216; concerns about concentrating the U.S. fleet at Pearl Harbor in the mid-1930s, p. 217

Pensacola, Florida
   Conditions for young officers in mid-1910s, pp. 10-11

Philippines
   As a child in the 1920s, Roy Smith III takes bones from Philippine burial cave as a souvenir, p. 167

Philippine Sea, Battle of
   Mitscher embarrassed by praise for decision to turn on carrier lights for returning pilots during action in June 1944, pp. 35-37

"Powder Monkeys"
   Fourteen-year-old Roy Smith III accompanies Lieutenant Commander Smith in Noa (DD-343) to Nanking in the mid-1920s, helping with the guns, pp. 94-95, 176

Read, Rear Admiral William A., USN
   Friendship between Mitschers and Reads, pp. 27-28

Richardson, Admiral James O., USN   (USNA, 1902)
   Future Commander in Chief U.S. Fleet complains about concentration of the fleet at Pearl Harbor in the mid-1930s, p. 217

Ritchie, Albert C.
   Maryland governor from 1920 to 1924 remembered for his wild parties, pp. 98-99

Rizal, USS (DD-174)
   Picks up Lieutenant Commander Smith in Shanghai in 1925 and takes him to his new command, the Noa (DD-343), p. 140

The Rodgers Family
   Discussion of Mrs. Smith's illustrious relatives, pp. 117-118, 120; See Captain William L. Rodgers, USN

Rodgers, Captain William L., USN   (USNA, 1878)
   As commanding officer of the Georgia (BB-15) in the early
   1910s, invites his cousin Mary Alger to a fancy wardroom
   dinner, pp. 225-226

Sherman, Vice Admiral Forrest P., USN   (USNA, 1918)
   Tours European naval installations with Mitscher in August
   1946, p. 3

Smith, Mary Taylor Alger
   Parents, pp. 64, 68, 76, 79, 86, 89, 123; schooling, pp. 74-
   76, 80; dates at the Naval Academy in the early 1900s, pp. 78,
   85-87, 89, 104, 108; ancestors and relatives, pp. 81, 109,
   114, 117-120; friends and childhood activities, pp. 70-73, 76-
   77, 80-82, 97, 99-100, 104-105, 113, 115, 225; meets and
   marries Roy Smith, Jr., in the early 1900s, pp. 104-105, 108-
   110, 120; rushes to Charleston in the early 1920s when she
   receives word that her husband is ill, pp. 133-134; Mrs.
   Smith's comic experiences with Chinamen in her bedroom, pp.
   143-144, 150-151, 154-155; alone with children in Far East
   from June 1925 to February 1928, pp. 140-174

Smith, Montgomery M.
   Friend of John Kane, Jr., pp. 116-117; born in Annapolis
   during 1919 flu epidemic, p. 131; health, pp. 164-165;
   education, pp. 210-211

Smith, Commander Roy C., Jr., USN (Ret.)   (USNA, 1910)
   Duty as commanding officer in Noa (DD-343) in China in the
   mid-1920s, pp. 94, 137-138, 140-141, 151; relatives and
   ancestors, pp. 95, 118-119; courts and marries Mary Alger in
   1912, pp. 104-105, 108-110, 114; duty in South Carolina (BB-
   26) during World War I, pp. 123, 226; service in merchant ship
   Luckenbach during World War II, pp. 123-126; educated abroad,
   p. 125; stationed at the Naval Academy during World War I, pp.
   126-127, 131; health, pp. 133-134, 211, 213, 220-223;
   commanding officer of USS King (DD-242) in early 1920s, p.
   133; stationed at the Naval Academy in 1922, initially
   rejected by superintendent, RADM Wilson, as undesirable, pp.
   135-137; takes command of Noa during typhoon, pp. 151-152;
   navigator in Memphis (CL-13) in the early 1930s, pp. 204, 211;
   translates at the Naval War College after retirement for
   health reasons in 1937, pp. 213-214; commanding officer of the
   Oglala (CM-4) in the mid-1930s, unhappy because he was not
   allowed to map Pacific area, pp. 216-221

Smith, Captain Roy C. III, USNR (Ret.)
   Resigns from the Naval Academy in December 1933 after running
   up demerits, pp. 71, 102, 207-208; wife and children, pp. 81,

211-212; tells sisters not to date his midshipmen friends in the early 1930s, pp. 88-89; as "powder monkey" in Noa (DD-343) in mid-1920s, pp. 93-95, 76; relatives and ancestors, pp. 95, 118-119, 62; born in 1913 while father at sea, pp. 120-121; scares Mrs. Smith by sneaking on train to Baltimore as young child, pp. 127-131; as child, takes bones as souvenir from Philippine burial cave, p. 167; education, pp. 178, 207

Social Activities
   Enjoyed by the Mitschers, pp. 12, 23-24, 44, 49; at the Naval Academy in the early 1900s, pp. 78-79, 87; at Newport in the 1920s-1940s, pp. 96-97, 101, 178-189, 191-198; in Annapolis in the early 1900s, pp. 98, 103, 115; in Shanghai in the mid-1920s, p. 155

Spanish-American War
   Mrs. Smith's recollections of her family's participation, p. 109

Staley, Mary Smith
   Sent back to States to get away from Panama climate in the early 1930s, p. 209; education, p. 211; stays in Hawaii with the Kenneth Whitings when her parents leave in 1937, pp. 211-223

Steichen, Lieutenant Commander Edward J., USNR
   Photographs Marc Mitscher in June 1944, p. 37

Taylor, Admiral Montgomery M., USN (USNA, 1890)
   Served with Admiral Dewey at the Battle of Manila Bay in 1898, p. 109; gives away his niece Mary Alger at her wedding in August 1912, p. 114; followed long family line in commanding Asiatic Fleet in the early 1930s, p. 117; tries to discourage Mrs. Smith from accompanying her husband to China in 1925, p. 137

Television
   Admiral Mitscher makes one of the first appearances by a naval officer on TV after World War II, pp. 2-3

Torpedo Squadron Eight
   Mitscher's reaction to the loss of this squadron during 1942 Midway action, pp. 58-59

Torpedo Station, Newport, Rhode Island
   Social activities in the late 1920s, pp. 90-91, 96-97, 101; description of housing, p. 177

Transatlantic Flight
    Mitscher's unsuccessful 1919 attempt in NC-1, pp. 29-31

Transportation
    Around Annapolis in the early 1900s, pp. 80, 110-111, 113; method of commuting to Washington from Annapolis in the early 1900s, pp. 110-111; Smith dependents taken to China aboard commercial ship in 1925, p. 139

Vanguard, HMS
    Last Royal Navy battleship severely damaged in storm in the 1950s, pp. 200-201

Whiting, Captain Kenneth, USN (USNA, 1905)
    As close friend of Marc Mitscher, pp. 45, 56; assessed by Mrs. Mitscher, pp. 56-57; Mary Smith stays with the Whitings in Hawaii in 1937, pp. 221-222; daughter remains friends with the Smiths, pp. 223-224

Williams, Admiral Clarence S., USN (USNA, 1884)
    As commander in chief of the Asiatic Fleet in the mid-1920s, refuses to allow Navy dependents to accompany men on ships, pp. 94, 176

Wilson, Rear Admiral Henry B., USN (USNA, 1881)
    As superintendent of the Naval Academy in 1922, opposes Lieutenant Commander Smith's orders to the Academy until shown there was a case of mistaken identity, pp. 135-136

World War I
    Influx of civilians into Navy brings about changed policy on transfer of dependents, p. 122; Navy wives suffered over news of ship sinkings without details, pp. 125-126; Lieutenant Smith disappointed at being stationed at the Naval Academy during war, pp. 126-127

www.ingramcontent.com/pod-product-compliance
Lightning Source LLC
Chambersburg PA
CBHW082204070526
44585CB00020B/2272